Proxy War in Yemen

This book analyzes the civil war in Yemen and how intervening external actors have shaped the trajectory of the conflict. The work examines the conflict in Yemen as a testing ground for expectations about the autonomy and control of proxies by external patrons and the direct consequences for civilian victimization and duration of war. Like other proxy wars, the international dimensions of the war made the conflict in Yemen subject to the geopolitical interests of intervening powers. The longstanding power rivalry between Saudi Arabia and Iran over Middle East supremacy resulted in a competitive intervention in Yemen, where the initial belligerents of the civil war—the Houthi and the Hadi regime—were used as proxies by Tehran and the Gulf coalition led by Riyadh, respectively. Their intervention ultimately translated into a prolonged and destructive conflict. The often contradictory and self-interested patronage strategies by the coalition's two central patrons, Saudi Arabia and the United Arab Emirates, undermined their broader goal of containing Iran. However, Iran's support for the Houthis enabled them to bait and bleed the Gulf coalition. Lastly, in an effort to balance against Iran, the United States underwrote the military campaign of the Gulf states with military hardware and personnel, thereby further prolonging the conflict and humanitarian disaster. This book concludes that intervention by external patrons both protracted the civil war and made it far more destructive for the civilian population.

This book will be of much interest to students of proxy wars, Middle Eastern conflict, and security studies in general.

Bernd Kaussler holds a PhD in International Relations from the University of St Andrews and is currently a Professor of Political Science at James Madison University. His recent scholarship includes *Rhetoric and Governance under Trump: Proclamations from the Bullshit Pulpit* (2020), *US Foreign Policy Towards the Middle East: The Realpolitik of Deceit* (2017), and *Iran's Nuclear Diplomacy: Power Politics and Conflict Resolution* (2014).

Keith A. Grant holds a PhD in Political Science from the University of Arizona and is currently an Associate Professor of Political Science at James Madison University. His research focuses on violent interstate conflict and international cooperation.

Cass Military Studies

Military Strategy of Great Powers
Managing Power Asymmetry and Structural Change in the 21st Century
Håkan Edström and Jacob Westberg

Counterinsurgency Warfare and Brutalisation
The Second Russian-Chechen War
Roberto Colombo and Emil Aslan Souleimanov

Managing Security
Concepts and Challenges
Edited by Laura R. Cleary and Roger Darby

Understanding the Impact of Social Research on the Military
Reflections and Critiques
Edited by Eyal Ben-Ari, Helena Carreiras, and Celso Castro

Civil-Military Cooperation in International Interventions
The Role of Soldiers
Agata Mazurkiewicz

Contemporary Military Reserves
Between the Civilian and Military Worlds
Edited by Eyal Ben-Ari and Vincent Connelly

Military Strategies of the New European Allies
A Comparative Study
Håkan Edström and Jacob Westberg

Proxy War in Yemen
Bernd Kaussler and Keith A. Grant

For more information about this series, please visit: https://www.routledge.com/Cass-Military-Studies/book-series/CMS

Proxy War in Yemen

Bernd Kaussler and
Keith A. Grant

LONDON AND NEW YORK

First published 2023
by Routledge
4 Park Square, Milton Park, Abingdon, Oxon OX14 4RN

and by Routledge
605 Third Avenue, New York, NY 10158

Routledge is an imprint of the Taylor & Francis Group, an informa business

© 2023 Bernd Kaussler and Keith A. Grant

The right of Bernd Kaussler and Keith A. Grant to be identified as authors of this work has been asserted in accordance with sections 77 and 78 of the Copyright, Designs and Patents Act 1988.

All rights reserved. No part of this book may be reprinted or reproduced or utilised in any form or by any electronic, mechanical, or other means, now known or hereafter invented, including photocopying and recording, or in any information storage or retrieval system, without permission in writing from the publishers.

Trademark notice: Product or corporate names may be trademarks or registered trademarks, and are used only for identification and explanation without intent to infringe.

British Library Cataloguing-in-Publication Data
A catalogue record for this book is available from the British Library

Library of Congress Cataloging-in-Publication Data
Names: Kaussler, Bernd, author. | Grant, Keith A., author.
Title: Proxy war in Yemen / Bernd Kaussler and Keith A. Grant.
Description: Abingdon, Oxon ; New York, NY : Routledge, [2023] | Series: Cass military studies | Includes bibliographical references and index.
Identifiers: LCCN 2022038488 (print) | LCCN 2022038489 (ebook) | ISBN 9781032201665 (hardback) | ISBN 9781032201764 (paperback) | ISBN 9781003262602 (ebook)
Subjects: LCSH: Yemen (Republic)--History--Civil War, 2015- | Yemen (Republic)--Politics and government--21st century. | Proxy war--History--21st century.
Classification: LCC DS247.Y48 K385 2023 (print) | LCC DS247.Y48 (ebook) | DDC 953.305/3--dc23/eng/20220812
LC record available at https://lccn.loc.gov/2022038488
LC ebook record available at https://lccn.loc.gov/2022038489

ISBN: 978-1-032-20166-5 (hbk)
ISBN: 978-1-032-20176-4 (pbk)
ISBN: 978-1-003-26260-2 (ebk)

DOI: 10.4324/9781003262602

Typeset in Times New Roman
by MPS Limited, Dehradun

Contents

1 Introduction 1

2 Proxy War: A Primer 5

3 Proxy War in the Middle East 23

4 Key Military Engagements in Yemen, 2014–2022 37

5 External Patrons of Surrogates in Yemen's Civil War 75

6 Conclusion 119

Index 124

1 Introduction

As the Arab Spring spread across the Middle East, an emboldened Yemeni population took to the streets to protest the repressive, widely corrupt government headed by President Ali Abdullah Saleh for more than three decades. The legislative and judicial branches had been subordinated beneath the executive branch. Nearly all top positions, including the prime minister and membership to the Supreme Judiciary Council, were filled through presidential appointment and heavily favored the president's family and other tribal or political elites loyal to Saleh. In response to widespread protests sweeping the country in 2011, President Saleh announces he will not see reelection following the end of his current term in 2013, and a process to return legislative powers to the elected parliament. As protests continue, the government response becomes more repressive culminating in the killing of at least 50 protestors by governmental security forces in civilian clothes in March 2011. Members of Parliament from Saleh's General People's Congress (GPC), Yemen's strongest political party at the time, resign *en masse* and political elites begin organizing against the president. In May, President Saleh agrees to resign from office, only to renege on that promise a few days later.

After narrowly surviving an assassination attempt in June 2011, presidential authority is temporarily transferred to Vice President Abd-Rabbu Mansour Hadi while Saleh receives medical treatment for his injuries in neighboring Saudi Arabia. He returns to Yemen three months later facing a fractured GPC and a more cohesive faction of opposition parties, coupled with continued mass unrest across the general population. Under considerable pressure from the Gulf Cooperation Council and the United Nations Security Council, President Saleh formally cedes power to Vice President Hadi on November 23, 2011 during a ceremony hosted by Saudi King Abdullah in Riyadh.

DOI: 10.4324/9781003262602-1

Hadi was a weak president. His ascension to the presidency ostensibly reflected Saudi interests and power more than they derived legitimacy from the Yemeni people. This was especially true in the North, where former President Saleh maintained considerable influence among the GPC and tribal leadership and bore resentment toward Hadi and other Yemeni elites who, in Saleh's view, had betrayed him. The northern governorates were also home to the Zaydis, a sect of Shia Islam constituting about one-third of the population of Yemen. The unification of Yemen in 1990 dramatically reduced the influence of the Zaydi population; they had constituted a majority in the North Yemen, but became a minority in unified Yemen as the South was predominantly Sunni. Furthermore, the composition of the transitional government, brokered by the Gulf States and especially Saudi Arabia, preserved the *ancien régime's* influence while further empowering the Saudi-linked Sunni party, al-Islah, a conservative Sunni party with ties to the Muslim Brotherhood and Saudi Arabia.

Ansar Allah, colloquially known as the Houthis, is a Zaydi Shia movement emerging during the 1990s, shortly after Yemeni unification. Originally, the Houthis opposed Saleh's government over its extreme corruption that enriched the elite while the general public remained impoverished and their belief that Yemeni government was too closely aligned with Saudi Arabia and the United States. The 2004 death of the movement's leader, Hussein Badreddin al-Houthi, by governmental security forces during an attempted arrest would push the movement toward violent rebellion and the adoption of the "Houthi" moniker. The next several years saw on-again-off-again violence between the Houthi, the government, and several pro-government tribal groups.

After more than a year in office, the Yemeni government led by Hadi failed to meaningfully address cronyism and corruption and did little to improve wellbeing of the general public. In early 2014, and at the behest of the International Monetary Fund, the government announces the end of the fuel subsidy program which would see the price of fuel increase by about 60%. Although elites could exploit these subsidies through smuggling government-subsidized fuel across borders to be sold at a profit, the consequences would disproportionately impact the poor general public as the price hike reverberated throughout the economy. The weakness of the Hadi government had allowed the Houthi to expand their membership and influence, while the end of fuel subsidies created a rally flag that mustered popular support. Massive protests during the summer would lead to the convergence of Houthi forces around the capital city, Sana'a, which would be under Houthi control by the end of September. As Houthi forces overtook the capital, the military fractured along tribal and personal loyalties. Some units mutinied, stood aside, and even besieged and fought against their compatriots. Former President Saleh, whose government had repressed the Houthi movement since the 1990s, had backed them. Efforts to reach a negotiated settlement failed, forcing Hadi's government to resign in January 2015. Hadi fled South to Aden, unresigned, and requested military assistance from Saudi Arabia. As the Battle of Aden began in March 2015, the ten-country coalition led by Saudi Arabia would launch Operation Decisive Storm, a month-long aerial campaign targeting Houthi forces and the Saleh-aligned factions of the Yemeni military that had sided with the Houthis as President Hadi fled to Saudi Arabia. During that first month of the coalition's intervention, air strikes against at least 503 targets resulted in no fewer than 651 fatalities; 48 of those air strikes, nearly 10%, are classified as civilian targets by the ACLED project.[1]

After seven years of war, the United Nations brokered a tenuous ceasefire going into effect on April 2, 2022. During that time, the United Nations estimates that at least 337,000 people have died because of the war,[2] with ACLED attributing 161,996 fatalities—combatant and civilian—to the conflict-related actions of the many belligerents participating in the violence.[3] The impact on civilians is staggering: more than four million Yemenis have been displaced by the conflict or have fled the country as refugees; over 20 million people representing about two-thirds of the country's population, half being children, are reported by UNICEF as in need of humanitarian relief.[4] War crimes, including the intentional targeting of civilians, are commonplace.

Project Outline

Chapter 2 provides the theoretical framework and surveys the most recent literature on proxy war, surrogate control and civilian victimization. As with most proxy wars, the war in Yemen also showed that patrons are pursuing larger geopolitical objectives and, therefore, view the conflict instrumentally, focusing on those larger goals rather than bringing about a decisive end to the fighting. In the Yemeni theater, this meant that the Saudi leadership pursued a maximalist position to reinstate the Hadi government at all costs, while Iran merely wanted to "bait and bleed" Saudis into a costly and lengthy asymmetrical war.

Chapter 3 shows how the invasion of Iraq by the United States in 2003 represented a systemic shock to the balance of power in the Middle East and ushered in decade of regional proxy war. The Arab Spring revolution-turned civil wars in Syria and Libya are recognized as important theaters in this trajectory. The contest for regional dominance between Saudi Arabia and Iran made Yemen the Middle East's latest proxy war.

Chapter 4 depicts and analyzes key battles in the civil war from September 2014 when Houthis took control of the capital until 2022 when the Biden administration announced that it would revoke the Houthis' designation as a terrorist group and ceased US support for "offensive Saudi operations". Drawing on qualitative and quantitative research, it focuses on Yemen's shifting military balance over the years.

Chapter 5 analyzes strategies and impact of external patrons Iran, Saudi Arabia, United Arab Emirates on the conflict. We term the United States a "super patron" as it used Saudi Arabia as means to off-shore balance against Iran. The chapter discusses patron control over proxies as well as how fissures within the coalition resulted in support of opposing proxies but also prolonged the conflict. Overall, we argue that the lack of hierarchy between Washington and Riyadh relations resulted in effectively unchecked Saudi behavior in Yemen.

Lastly, we conclude that the intervention by external patrons both protracted the civil war and made it far more destructive for the civilian population. Supply lines from the United States to Saudi Arabia and from Iran to Houthis caused an ongoing military stalemate in which none of the belligerents were able to decisively win the conflict. While Houthis largely emerged as the dominant belligerent with regards to control of territory as well as offensive posture toward Saudi Arabia, a political settlement remained elusive. The Obama, Trump, and Biden administrations maintained a largely unconditional position toward Saudi Arabia's military operations, therefore, underwriting the extensive military hardware required for an eight-year-long war.

Notes

1 Clionadh Raleigh, Andrew Linke, Håvard Hegre and Joakim Karlsen (2010). "Introducing ACLED: An Armed Conflict Location and Event Dataset: Special Data Feature". *Journal of Peace Research* 47 (5): 651–60.
2 Taylor Hanna, David K. Boyd, and Jonathan D. Moyer (2021). *Assessing the Impact of War in Yemen: Pathways for Recovery.* United Nations Development Programme, https://www.undp.org/publications/assessing-impact-war-yemen-pathways-recovery
3 We adopt the UN brokered ceasefire entering effect on April 2, 2022 as our cut-off date for any figures or analyses using the ACLED data. Unfortunately, despite the ceasefire, some political violence continues.
4 UNICEF (2022). "Yemen Appeal", https://www.unicef.org/appeals/yemen (accessed 16 June 2022).

2 Proxy War: A Primer

Introduction

In May 2022, media outlets in the United States reported that the United States had provided logistical support to Ukrainian defense forces including targeting information on Russian mobile command centers that had facilitated the targeting and killing of multiple Russian generals, shifting the nature of American logistical support from defensive to potentially offensive. Additionally, US Secretary of Defense Lloyd Austin had previously stated the United States' interest in "see[ing] Russia weakened to the degree it cannot do the kinds of things that it has done in Ukraine".[1] While the Biden administration insisted that the United States had not entered a proxy war against Russia, it had stated an objective for the conflict that was larger than the defense of Ukraine alone and had provided Ukrainian defense forces logistical and material support, including drones capable of targeting individuals, which were arguably better suited toward the strategic weakening of the Russian military than to the immediate defense of Ukraine.

Recent and ongoing conflicts including the civil war in Syria, US operations in Afghanistan and Iraq, NATO involvement in Libya, Russian sponsorship of rebels in Donbas, Ukraine, and the civil war in Yemen have all drawn the moniker of *proxy war* by the media, analysts, policymakers, and academics. Yet there remains some ambiguity as to what the term means.[2] In the common vernacular, the term *proxy war* often carries a negative connotation and is generally understood through the lens of the US-Soviet superpower rivalry. During the cold war, local belligerents in proxy wars were perceived as "pawns" being used by the external powers, forced to subordinate their own interests to those of the intervening powers and thus minimizing or even eliminating local agency over the conflict's trajectory. It appears that this connotation may carry into the academic literature on proxy war and

DOI: 10.4324/9781003262602-2

tangential topics, especially noticeable in the variations in terminology used across the literature to both identify and describe the actors' positions as well as the phenomenon more broadly. For example, Rauta's analysis of terminology used throughout the academic literature on proxy war finds 11 common terms used to label the local actor: "client", "pawn", "proxy", "pseudo-volunteers", "puppet", "satellite", "subordinate", "surrogate", "superclient", "tool", and "volunteer".[3] Moreover, the compartmentalization of the international relations discipline, often along theoretical and methodological lines, has led to parallel literatures emerging, with a primarily qualitative and conceptual literature focusing on "proxy war" and a more quantitative and empirical literature investigating "conflict delegation" that have not engaged one another until recently.[4]

Despite this ambiguity, the renewed interest in conflict through proxy reflects the belief that direct, violent conflict between states has decreased in frequency and intensity,[5] internal conflict is rare, and the dominant form of political violence remains intrastate, where a rebel group squares off against the government, usually for control of the country.[6] A plurality of intrastate wars—and indeed about two-thirds of rebel groups—receives some form of material assistance from external states.[7] The presence of external support for one or more of the disputants tends increase the duration[8] and severity of the conflict, resulting in higher human costs especially among the civilian population of a country experiencing internal conflict.[9]

Defining Proxy War

Mumford's (2013) definition of a proxy war as "conflicts in which a third party intervenes indirectly in order to influence the strategic outcome in favour of its preferred faction" is a commonly referenced definition that provides a useful entry point.[10] Mumford further elaborates that "benefactor" can channel support into a conflict through a chosen proxy, which allows the external party to avoid the costs associated with direct intervention in a conflict. Central to his approach is the *indirect* nature of the external involvement – material assistance including weapons, logistical support, training, and funding – replace direct participation in combat operations as avoiding the costs or consequences of such involvement is a driving factor in a state's decision to engage via proxy. The conceptualization is both transactional and hierarchical, as the benefactor "hires" the proxy to engage in subterfuge on its behalf. Pfaff expands upon this conceptualization, adding that some direct involvement of the benefactor does not necessarily preclude a proxy relationship if forms of assistance are used to substitute for a direct action that the benefactor would otherwise undertake themselves in support of their proxy.[11] He uses the example of coalition air strikes against governmental targets coupled with material support for Libyan rebel groups (proxies) on the ground. The air strikes were a direct support operation, but the material assistance enabled the substitution of local forces for otherwise necessary coalition forces, thereby minimizing risk and costs to the benefactors. Hughes (2012) echoes the hierarchical relational dynamic of proxy war, emphasizing strategic the use of third parties as either a substitute for or augmentation on benefactor's own efforts.[12] A managerial aspect is added by Groh (2019), who defines proxy war as an external actor "directing the use of force by a politically motivated, local actor to indirectly influence political affairs in the target state".[13] This differentiates between proxy war and what he terms "donated assistance", a separate form of indirect intervention where the intervening state does not intentionally or actively shape how those resources are used.

Surrogate warfare, as defined by Krieg and Rickli (2019), is "[t]he externalization ... of the strategic, operational, and tactical burden of war to human or technological surrogates with the principal intent of minimizing the patron's own burden of war".[14] Surrogate warfare is presented as a broader form of indirect conflict in which the patron seeks to conceal its own involvement and responsibility from public scrutiny. War through proxy is one option from a playbook including deployment of cyberweapons, targeted strikes by unmanned drones, troll-farm propaganda campaigns, employment of private military contractors to name a few of the less creative techniques. Interestingly, though Krieg and Rickli go to great lengths to present surrogate warfare as conceptually distinct from a proxy war, yet their inclusion of various technologies as cyberattacks "surrogates" largely mirrors Mumford's description[15] albeit with the caveat that Krieg and Rickli reference the technology itself as the "surrogate" while Mumford is suggesting the use of a third-party proxy to use the technology.

The term "conflict delegation" is often used in the quantitative literature to denote a form of indirect interstate conflict distinct from more traditional conflict intervention as the intervening third party has some degree of influence or control over the conflict's objectives and execution, thus injecting an external interest into the central incompatibility at the core of the underlying conflict.[16] This injects at least one likely more powerful actor with interests partially external to the conflict into the bargaining process. Here, the difference in terminology might be more meaningful; because "conflict delegation" is most prevalent in the quantitative literature, relying heavily on existing datasets for empirical testing, it is often an assumption rather than an observation of the intervening party's conflict role and purpose. When such intervention happens on opposing sides of a civil war, it becomes "competitive intervention", defined as "two-sided, simultaneous military assistance from different third-party states to both government and rebel combatants".[17] This conceptualization emphasized the external bargaining game between multiple intervening parties and the impact it has on the subject conflict.

Despite the variety in terminology used throughout the proxy war literature, both in the core concept itself as well as the meaning of the structural and relational roles actors undertake (e.g., benefactor, patron, sponsor, principal, client, proxy, surrogate, etc.), the common theoretical threads prevailing through the subject seem to be the importance of the third party's intervention to the local disputant's capabilities, the interest of the third party being at least in part exogenous to the central issue of the conflict, and the indirect, hierarchical nature of the relationship between patron and proxy. In Yemen, we observe each of these three requisites. For example, weapons transfer from Iran to Houthi forces greatly expanded Houthi offensive capability, notably allowing them to directly threaten Saudi infrastructure as the war continued (chapter 5). Likewise, coalition air strikes were central to pro-regime forces efforts to retake Houdeidah, an important port city, from Houthi control (chapter 4).

The Patron-Proxy Relationship

The strategic relationship between patron and proxy is almost universally presented as a principal-agent relationship in which the principal empowers its agent to work on its behalf, a common example being a legislator (agent) being elected to represent their constituents (principals) in the national legislature. The relationship is hierarchical in that the principal's power or authority is delegated to the agent to wield. To the extent that principal and agent interests align, this delegation is not problematic. However, as interests diverge, the agent will have an incentive to leverage the principal's resources toward its own objectives, while the principal carries the risk of being exploited by the agent. Generally, the agent will have an informational advantage. It likely has a superior understanding of the local strategic environment and it almost certainly better comprehends the degree of similarity or divergence of the principal's interests from its own. The principal's goals cannot be met if they are not communicated fully to the agent, while an agent with divergent or supplementary objectives has an incentive to obscure or misrepresent their own interests to increase their chances of being selected by the principal. Further, the agent also better understands its capabilities vis-à-vis the objective, though may have an incentive to misrepresent those capabilities to gain access the principal's delegated resources and authority.

In the proxy war context, an emerging conflict presents an opportunity for an external actor to pursue an interest at reduced cost through sponsorship of an already active belligerent in that conflict. The third party is usually but not always a state, while the proxy is usually but not always a non-state actor.[18] The conflict itself is a means for the patron to secure its interests through the proxy, adding the important caveat that the patron is not always interested in the proxy's ultimate success.[19] Iran's support for the Houthis provides a good example, as Iran's motivation for backing Houthi forces was to force Gulf states to expend resources over a long and protracted conflict, weakening them in the long term. In this context, a decisive Houthi victory would work against Iranian strategic interests. Rather, sponsorship of the proxy provides the patron with an intermediate approach when the repercussions of inaction are perceived as high, but direct intervention would be restrictively costly.[20] Frequently, these costs are domestic audience costs stemming from a public that might be war-wary or otherwise opposed to direct involvement by creating an emotional buffer between the general public and the acts of violence being conducted on the state's behalf. For example, casualties to private military contractors or sponsored insurgent groups will not be as noticeable or carry the same weight as repatriated servicemembers.[21] Moreover, war atrocities and crimes including the purposeful targeting of civilian populations fall on the proxy rather than the patron, providing an operator to do the dirty work that a government is unwilling to do itself.[22] Use of proxies can additionally make up for a shortcoming in the patron's capability, provide an advantage of local knowledge, or avoid legitimacy concerns that might arise with more direct intervention.

Of course, the employment of proxies is not without risks, both domestic and foreign. At home, democratic patrons especially will need to "manage" their general public's perception of the intervention. On the one hand, this requires establishing a justifiable pretext for intervention, which can be difficult when an overt domestic connection (such as kinship or a cultural tie) is absent; oftentimes, democracies will reference "human rights violations" to justify interventions when interests are more difficult for the public to observe.[23] However, when a strong tie between the patron's public and the proxy does exist, the political costs of abandonment may be increased, making it difficult for a patron to abandon an unsuccessful operation. In other contexts, intervention through proxy can obscure participation in a conflict from an inattentive public's eye. There would be little tolerance for extended US involvement in war in the Middle East; however, material support for its "allies" and "partners", military training and advising, logistical support, and weapons transfers is all but entirely invisible to the public's eye unless their attention is drawn by some major shock. This is exemplified in chapter 5, where an American congressional staffer states that very bluntly legislators are uninterested in the US's involvement in Yemen because American voters generally do not care. Additionally, though intervention through proxy is typically a means of limiting the risks of escalation with the target, conflicts often see "competitive intervention", where patrons supporting opposing sides enter a difficult balancing game where each seeks to maximize support to their own proxy without either crossing the line into direct confrontation or prompting the opposing patron to respond with support to their own proxy that would offset the former's contribution.[24] These competitive intervention scenarios can make victory fleeting, leading to the "don't lose" approach common to many partisan third party intervention in civil wars.

The proxy typically enters the patron-proxy relationship to overcome some deficiency in capabilities. Compared to their patrons, they generally have an advantage in local knowledge and information, including knowledge of the terrain, culture, and language. They are also likely to carry some legitimacy among the local population, increasing their ability to function in general, mobilize support, and govern if eventually victorious.[25] However, non-state proxies especially often lack the training and equipment needed to make meaningful gains in the conflict, opening them to adopt an external actor's goals as their own in exchange for the material and logistical assistance needed to pursue those objectives. The proxy's ability to pursue its own objectives may be inhibited in at least two ways. First, there may be a legitimacy cost for the proxy—especially if their overall goal is to govern—in needing external assistance while additionally subjugating their interests, at least in part, to those of the patron. Finally, the provision of assistance from the patron does not come free of strings; sufficient progress toward the patron's goal, or at least the semblance of progress, is likely a condition of continuing patronage. In Yemen, the Hadi government lost nearly all legitimacy through its dependence on the Saudi-led coalition for survival. Hadi was president in name only, clearly serving at the pleasure of Saudi Arabia, and his government was easily cast aside by the Saudis in 2022 when it no longer furthered their interests.

Control in the Proxy-Patron Relationship

Establishing a proxy relationship rather than "donating assistance" indicates the patron's desire or need to maintain a degree of control over the proxy, most likely due to divergent goals and interests. When the interests of the patron and proxy align perfectly, there is no continued need for the patron's involvement as provisioning the proxy with adequate capabilities to achieve the shared objective will deliver to the patron it's desired outcome. More frequently, the patron's interests are at least partially external to the proxy's underlying conflict and likely not central to the proxy's interests in prevailing in the current conflict. Depending on the nature of the national interest at stake, Groh suggests four proxy war strategies adopted by patrons which not only shape the proxy-patron relationship but also differentiate indirect interventions (proxy war and donated assistance) from non-intervention and direct intervention.[26] States will opt for direct military intervention when vital national interests are clearly at stake affecting the state's survival or security, or when there is the possibility of exceedingly desirable strategic gains sufficient to offset the risks. Below this threshold is the realm of indirect intervention, which applies to combinations of moderate vital and desirable interests. Here, the combination of risks and rewards to the patron governs the implemented approach to indirect intervention. They might provide more unlimited assistance when achieving victory is significant to interests and risks of counter-intervention are limited. As salience decreases or risks increase, patrons may view conflict victory as a secondary prize to either extending the current favorable status quo or imposing meddlesome costs on an opponent in a low-risk manner. Finally, in some instances, the patron might be apathetic or even opposed to the conflict outcome, seeking only to impose costs on the target through whatever means possible. In these proverbial *bait-and-bleed* situations, the proxy's ability to achieve its goal requires it to act independently and perhaps against the interests of its patron.

The principal-agent framework generally suggests a power asymmetry that favors the external principal and an information asymmetry that favors the local proxy. The proxy has the more complete understanding of both parties' interests, better understands the local strategic environment, and has an advantage in its ability to act within that environment.[27] But the proxy also lacks the capability needed to successfully pursue its goals without assistance. These asymmetries in addition to divergent objectives create an emergent *control—autonomy* dynamic wherein the proxy attempts to shift resources toward its objectives while the patron accounts for this possible defection through conditionalities, punishments, and rewards. In the patron's ideal scenario, the proxy's interests would be completely compatible with the patron's, eliminating fears of agency slack permitting a direct capacity building arrangement.[28] On the other hand, the proxy's informational advantage allows it to misrepresent its own interests to create a perception of converging interests to that end, hoping to maximize its ability to autonomously pursue its goals through the resource support provided by the patron. Knowing this, a wise patron should impose constraints on access to and usage of provisioned capabilities to avoid this moral hazard and create dependence as a means of controlling the proxy.

The most obvious strategy is to limit the proxy's access to weaponry through a slow and steady transfer of capability so that the proxy's degree of dependence is constant and tied to their effectiveness in conflict; up front provisioning of a proxy increases the proxy's autonomy to do as it sees fit with those resources, less dependent on the continued support of the patron and thus less constrained by the patron's interests.[29] By transforming the patron-proxy relationship from a single-transaction to a series of iterative transactions, the prisoner's dilemma-like incentive for the proxy to defect can be mitigated.[30] Common strategies employed in proxy relationships include embedding representatives within the proxy's command structure or deployed units, institutional checks on operational parameters (such as targeting), or gradual provisions of equipment and armaments to create a capable yet dependent proxy able to continue fighting but unable to do so without the support of the patron. Rewards and punishments that are tailored to the situation, specific in terms, and attainable can significantly increase patron-proxy cohesion.[31] Yet these approaches also entail risks. The need for continuous weapons transfers throughout the conflict risks supply disruptions both internal and external to the conflict. For example, the target will likely attempt to hinder those transfers by targeting shipments, establishing blockades, or signaling to the patron that continuance will be viewed as aggression. In Yemen, the need to control the major port city of Houdeidah led to an extended campaign, while both coalition and Houthi forces targeted the other's efforts to transport resources into Yemen by sea. Shifts in the patron's local security environment may also force reallocation of resources from the proxy operation to the patron's defense. The patron's domestic population may impose audience costs on the patron's government if their support is perceived to enable misbehavior such as indiscriminate or purposeful violence against civilians, problematizing future transfers due to rising scrutiny on the relationship. For example, the temporary attention to the United States' enablement of Saudi war crimes led to a brief rebuke of the Trump Administration's support to the kingdom, resulting in (vetoed) legislation requiring the cessation of that support.

Alternative Proxies and Patron Coalitions

The complexity inherent to contemporary civil war further complicates the management of patron-proxy relationships. Not only are civil wars more often than not internationalized, with at least one primary belligerent receiving direct assistance from an outside party, the domestic actors participating in intrastate conflict are not limited to a unified governmental force fighting against a monolith rebel group.[32] Pro-government militias, supporting and coordinating with the regime yet operating independently from it, are becoming increasingly common.[33] Likewise, there may also be a crowded field of patrons either working together as a coalition, separately for their own purposes, or some combination of the two.[34] The presence of multiple available patrons provides proxies with more autonomy, as patrons must outbid their counterparts to receive and retain the proxy's services. Accordingly, proxies extract more resources from patrons yet are less constrained in how those resources are used as patrons may now be substitutable. On the other hand, a crowded field of potential proxies increases the patron's authority, as the patron can credibly threaten to select a new proxy if its current proxy diverges too much from the patron's interests.[35] Given varying degrees of cohesion between paired patron and proxy interests and the informational advantage of the proxy, the patron sometimes "overpays" its proxy for fear of missing out on that proxy, either through increased resources or greater leeway in how those resources they are used.

The dynamics of patron coalitions further complicate matters. A multi-state coalition might form to coordinate efforts towards a larger shared goal, pool resources, reduce costs, and ensure a coordinated strategy.[36] In Yemen, the Saudis managed the air campaign against Houthi forces while UAE oversaw much of the on-the-ground intervention. Yet coalitions are political institutions that aggregate their members' interests towards a common interest; they are not devoid of disagreement or competing interests. Each coalition member faces different constraints through domestic audience costs[37] through which leaders are accountable to their selectorate[38] for the implications of their foreign policy actions. These domestic pressures are not always consistent and may vary by regime type. In democracies, leaders need to consider a larger selectorate comprised of the general public, which likely consists of minimizing risk and costs, avoiding casualties (especially civilian), and maintaining international reputation.[39] Democratic leaders will need to justify the costs of the intervention by establishing the salience of the security interest at stake or through minimizing awareness of its involvement by through a prominent role in the coalition at the expense of control. Autocratic states have smaller selectorates, though still face audience costs according to the elites' interest in the outcome and their ability to meaningfully coordinate to punish leadership for negative outcomes.[40] When the issue is highly salient, smaller selectorates permit fewer constraints on casualties or the targeting of civilians but likely a higher weight on outcome; the outcome itself will satisfy many members of the selectorate and those dissatisfied with the methods used to secure the outcome can be brought into the winning coalition through side payments. As a conflict progresses, mixed-regime coalitions especially may fissure as the strategy for prevailing in the conflict is likely not compatible with casualty and cost minimization. Less cohesion in the coalition increases proxy autonomy because on-the-ground proxies could threaten to defect to a new patron if terms are too strict, possibly increasing support and removing operational constraints.

Conflict Resolution, Severity, and Proxy War

Proxy war is often discussed from the vantage point of the patron – a proxy war occurs when an external party seeks to influence an ongoing conflict in their preferred manner acting through others. It is typically viewed as a hierarchical relationship where the intervening third party is the subject who acts, the proxy is the object used to manifest the action, and the war itself is the context in which this interaction occurs. This orients the bulk of the literature around the strategic reasons a patron would employ proxy war rather than direct intervention, the domestic, international, and material constraints that favor use of proxies, and the methods patrons can use to control proxies and prevent them from straying too far from the sponsor's goals. The prevalence of the principal-agent conceptualization of the patron-proxy interaction overemphasizes the patron's interests, role, and agency while dramatically reducing the agency to the proxy.[41]

The asymmetric conceptualization of the transaction is problematic for several reasons. First, it overlooks the origins and trajectory of the conflict by minimizing the relevance of the central grievances fueling the initial political violence. With the exception perhaps of private military contractors, the groups employed as proxies are almost always active in the conflict before the external sponsors.[42] Without negating the impact intervening third parties on the trajectory and outcome of conflicts, it is easy to forget that the underlying conflict exists independent of the proxy war component while the proxy component almost certainly does not exist separate from the underlying dispute. Second, the hierarchical conceptualization of the patron-proxy relationship assumes that the former possessing capital is superior to the latter providing labor. The relationship might be more accurately described as a mutually beneficial symbiosis between proxy and patron, and in Yemen it seems that the more horizontal Houhti-Iranian arrangement was more effective than the coalition's more vertical position visà-vis pro-Hadi forces.[43] In emphasizing how the patron's resources help the proxy overcome a relative disadvantage in capabilities, the patron's own weakness or constraints, whether it be operational, material, or resolve, are overlooked. The patron cannot achieve its goals independently (within tolerable cost constraints) any more so than the proxy can its own.

Finally, and most critically, portraying proxy war as a strategy savvy actors use to manage risk and reduce costs ignores that neither risk nor costs are reduced; they are instead transferred unto others. This relegates the very real human suffering to an afterthought of a strategic calculation as the conflict itself is viewed as an instrument, especially when the patron's goal is to bait and bleed its target in a prolonged and costly war, which maximizes human suffering. We acknowledge this trend in our own work, though we also attempt to emphasize the local, human costs of indirect, third party interventions and the incomprehensible human suffering patrons create when internationalizing an internal conflict in this manner.

Actor Complexity, Conflict Bargaining, and Conflict Severity

War is often conceptualized using a bargaining framework[44] that presents war as the inability of two opposed actors to agree upon the likely outcome of the conflict *ex ante* due to incomplete information they cannot (or should not) reveal regarding capabilities and/or resolve. Conflict becomes a costly means of revealing this information, permitting the disputants' understanding of these factors through violence. Uncertainty over rebel group capabilities is a common example. Most rebel organizations do not have public budgets or membership lists, nor do they procure weapons through conventional channels, allowing them to easily conceal and misrepresent their actual capabilities prior to conflict especially since it is almost certain that the balance of power significantly favors the government. Smuggling networks exploited by Yemeni elites throughout the Saleh regime would become valuable supply lines for Houthi forces. Second, a settlement short of victory would likely be conditional on rebels disarming and demobilizing, creating a commitment problem; nothing prevents the government from reneging on the agreement once rebels disarm and are unable to resist. Additionally, underlying issues in intrastate conflicts often involve both tangible and intangible components—for example, political and economic repression that intersects with identity—which contributes to interest incompatibility and issue indivisibility.

Civil wars are also often conceptualized as dyadic events where a rebel organization takes up arms against a government. Yet civil wars are almost always more complex making the common perception of unitary interests problematic.[45] Opposition movements may appear dominated by a specific group while actually being comprised of multiple distinct factions with distinct grievances, interests, and capabilities. Interests within the opposition may not always be fully compatible if the alliance is one of convenience in face of a common enemy rather than one of unified values or interests. Opposition to the Houthis created a common interest for Hadi loyalists in the North and anti-Houthi forces in the South yet a desire for succession would lead to confrontations between Hadi and the Southern Transitional Council. Conflict bargaining between the government and opposition becomes inherently more difficult because the opposition faction must first solve an internal coordination problem before settling with the government. The government may also seek to negotiate separately with factions, offering concessions regarding its interests as a payment for defecting from the opposition coalition. On the government side, pro-government militias have operated in 81% of internal conflicts between 1981 and 2014.[46] These militias are tactically less constrained than the governments they support because unlike the government itself, PGMs do not need to govern post-war. Pro-government militias supporting a government can commit atrocities on the government's behalf, especially against civilian populations, while buffering the government from liability for those actions.[47]

External actors contribute another degree of complexity when they intervene directly in conflict. Third party direct intervention favoring opposition groups can partially make up for the power deficit rebel groups experience via-à-vis the regime, moving the distribution of power closer to parity, thus rendering the conflict more difficult to resolve.[48] Pro-regime direct intervention tends to be less common, albeit because the conflict's internal balance generally favors the regime and there may be legitimacy losses were the regime unable to defeat a weaker, less organized opposition force without aid.[49] Pro-regime direct intervention seems conditional on the internal distribution of power and often reflects a negative shift in momentum where the regime's ability to prevail is in question. Regardless of side, third-party direct intervention rarely produces a decisive victory, but rather serves to prevent decisive defeat. When losing ground, whether it be physical territory or prospects of victory, primary belligerents tend to use increasingly indiscriminate means to avoid their worst-case outcome with civilians particularly at risk.[50] Third party interventions during declining momentum are similarly dangerous for civilians. Unlike domestic belligerents who are fighting for control of the country, intervening third parties show little need to prioritize civilian safety as they will not need local civilian support to govern tomorrow, leaving few costs other than possible domestic audience costs to deter negligent purposeful targeting of civilian bystanders.[51] As mentioned earlier, in proxy wars it can often be against the interests of the patron for the conflict to conclude.

Indirect third-party intervention through sponsorship and support of a proxy adds many of the same dynamics as direct intervention, with at least three additional impacts that reduce the likelihood of settlement and enhance conflict severity and lethality. One of the advantages of the proxy war approach for both patrons and proxies is deniability. Patrons can maintain a degree of separation from local actors and events. By providing weapons and other support covertly, patrons can shield themselves from domestic and international accountability for atrocities committed with those weapons despite their continued provisioning of the proxy as tacit support for those actions.[52] They might also seek to obscure their involvement form international actors as to either not appear aggressive or to not prompt escalation from an adversary in the "competitive intervention" model. Questions regarding Iran's material support to Houthis through 2017 exemplify this. Iranian officials maintain their early support to Houthis was spiritual and symbolic, and despite widespread allegations of Iranian weapons transfers prior to 2017, it is not until remnants of Houthi-fired missiles indicate Iranian origin that there is conclusive evidence of their active underwriting of Houthis. The commonality of multiple local actors in civil wars including pro-government militias and competing factions of the opposition likely that a proxy willing to act indiscriminately in pursuit of its (and the patron's) goals while the patron avoids blowback associated with flagrant violence. Targeting civilians, whether intentional or negligent, becomes more likely.

Next, patrons are not simply donating aid. They enter a patron-proxy relationship in order to maintain some degree of control over the proxy to offset possible agency slack and avoid outcomes that might impact the patron negatively. On the one hand, this adds additional voices into the conflict bargaining process, possibly preventing settlement between the primary actors. Were the government and opposition to find a mutually agreeable settlement, what guarantee is that that the patron will cease its support of another local actor if its own goals are not met?[53] As Groh discusses at length, a successful proxy war does not necessarily require the supported side to win; sowing chaos to impose costs on an enemy may have been the patron's primary motivation for intervening.[54] Patrons could also act as spoilers, preventing local actors from reaching or implementing a negotiated settlement. On the other hand, patrons that are able to address their objectives through bargaining are not able to guarantee that their proxies will cease hostilities, and as mentioned earlier, proxies may have the ability to "shop around" for a new patron to continue fighting. As discussed earlier, the bilateral bargaining process in civil war is inherently more complex than in interstate war. Additional actors with divergent preferences only make bargained settlement less feasible. Yet, the additional capabilities introduced to the conflict environment and the "don't lose" pattern of external intervention can block settlement through victory also, resulting in a conflict that is longer and more severe.

Finally, conflict zones are not known for their orderly and effective local governance, and war-torn countries face a multitude of challenges external to but caused by the war including lack of access to food, potable water, basic utilities, and economic opportunity to name a few. Belligerents in intrastate war often rely on extracting resources from the local community, if not voluntarily then through force.[55] Scarce resources compound human suffering and non-existent governance, leading to competition for resource access within and between local communities. Complex societal configurations, where local loyalties such as tribal affiliation are dominant, create opportunities for crime and violence along existing political or identity-based lines. This mirrors the expanded issue of in-fighting between factions of complex, loose coalitions.[56] Yemeni tribes were observed to have fought against one another nearly as often as they did against the Houthis. Furthermore, moving weapons and other supplies into and across a contemporary conflict zone is not a simple matter and often relies on unscrupulous methods including use of smugglers and other groups functioning outside the boundaries of legitimate commerce. Though not necessarily a direct result of the conflict, the perpetuated conflict enables unfettered criminal activity only worsening the already dire plight of those caught in the crossfire.

Notes

1 Julian E. Barnes, Helene Cooper, and Eric Schmitt, "US Intelligence Is Helping Ukraine Kill Russian Generals, Officials Say". *The New York Times* (4 May 2022), https://www.nytimes.com/2022/05/04/us/politics/russia-generals-killed-ukraine.html
2 See, for example, Idean Salehyan (2010). "The Delegation of War to Rebel Organizations". *Journal of Conflict Resolution* 54 (3): 493–515; Reinoud Leenders and Antonio Giustozzi, "Foreign Sponsorship of Progovernment Militias Fighting Syria's Insurgency: Whither Proxy Wars?". *Mediterranean Politics* (24 November 2020).
3 Vladimir Rauta (2018). "A Structural-Relational Analysis of Party Dynamics in Proxy Wars". *International Relations* 32 (4): 449–67, p. 453.
4 A 2021 forum focused on bridging this apparent gap. See Niklas Karlén et al. (2021). "Forum: Conflict Delegation in Civil Wars". *International Studies Review* 23: 2048–78.
5 Fazal and Poast provide an accessible and informative criticism of this perspective in a *Foreign Affairs* article: see Tanisha M. Fazal and Paul Poast (2019). "War Is Not Over: What the Optimists Get Wrong about Conflict". *Foreign Affairs* 98 (6): 74–83.
6 Therése Pettersson, Shawn Davies, Amber Deniz, Garoun Engström, Nanar Hawach, Stina Högbladh, and Margareta Sollenberg Magnus Öberg (2021). "Organized Violence 1989–2020, with a Special Emphasis on Syria". *Journal of Peace Research* 58 (4) 809–25.
7 Salehyan 2010; Belgin San-Acka (2016). *States in Disguise: Causes of State Support for Rebel Groups.* Oxford University Press.
8 See, for example, Dylan Balch-Lindsay and Andrew J. Enterline (2000). "Killing Time: The World Politics of Civil War Duration, 1820–1992". *International Studies Quarterly* 44 (4): 615–42; Patrick M. Regan (2002). "Third-Party Interventions and the Duration of Intrastate Conflicts". *The Journal of Conflict Resolution* 46 (1): 55–73; Paul Collier, Anke Hoeffler, and Måns Söderbom (2004). "On the Duration of Civil War". *Journal of Peace Research* 41 (3): 253–73; and David E. Cunningham (2010). "Blocking Resolution: How External States Can Prolong Civil Wars". *Journal of Peace Research* 47 (2): 115–27.
9 Idean Saleyhan, David Sikroy, and Reed Wood (2014). "External Rebel Sponsorship and Civilian Abuse: A Principal-Agent Analysis of Wartime Atrocities". *International Organization* 68 (3): 633–61; Laia Balcells and Stathis N. Kalyvas (2014). "Does Warfare Matter? Severity, Duration, and Outcomes of Civil Wars". *Journal of Conflict Resolution* 58 (8): 1390–418;

Huseyn Aliyev (2019). "Why Are Some Civil Wars More Lethal Than Others? The Effect of Pro-Regime Proxies on Conflict Lethality". *Political Studies* 68 (3): 749–67; Keith A. Grant and Bernd Kaussler (2020). "The Battle of Aleppo: External Patrons and the Victimization of Civilians in Civil War". *Small Wars and Insurgencies* 31 (1): 1–33.
10 Andrew Mumford (2013). "Proxy Warfare and the Future of Conflict". *The RUSI Journal* 158 (2): 40–46, p. 40.
11 C. Anthony Pfaff (2017). "Strategic Insights: Proxy War Norms". *Articles & Editorials* 402, https://press.armywarcollege.edu/articles_editorials/402
12 Geraint Hughes (2012). *My Enemy's Enemy: Proxy Warfare in International Politics.* Sussex Academic Press, p. 2.
13 Tyrone L. Groh (2019). *Proxy War: The Least Bad Option.* Stanford University Press, pp. 2–3.
14 Andreas Krieg and Jean-Marc Rickli (2019). *Surrogate Warfare: The Transformation of War in the Twenty-First Century.* Georgetown University Press, p. 58.
15 Mumford 2013, p. 43.
16 Salehyan 2010, p. 501, serves as the primary reference for the quantitative conceptualization of "conflict delegation".
17 Noel Anderson (2019). "Competitive Intervention, Protracted Conflict, and the Global Prevalence of Civil War". *International Studies Quarterly* 63: 692–706, p. 692.
18 For example, non-state actors such as al Qaeda and the Islamic State have recently employed proxies in multiple conflicts. See Assaf Morgadam and Michael Wyss (2020). "The Political Power of Proxies: Why Nonstate Actors Use Local Surrogates". *International Security* 44 (4): 119–57.
19 Groh 2019.
20 This cost-reduction argument is ubiquitous in the proxy war literature. See Salehyan 2010; Mumford 2013; Krieg and Rickli 2019; Groh 2019, and others.
21 Mumford 2013; Krieg and Rickli 2019.
22 Huseyn Ailyev (2019). "Why Are Some Civil Wars More Lethal Than Others? The Effect of Pro-Regime Proxies on Conflict Lethality". *Political Studies* 68 (3): 749–67.
23 Groh 2019, chapter 4.
24 Anderson 2019.
25 Salehyan 2010.
26 Groh 2019, chapter 2.
27 Salehyan 2010; Groh 2019. Eli Berman, Davis A. Lake, Gerard Padró i Miquel, and Pierre Yared (2019). "Principals, Agents, and Indirect Foreign Policies". In Eli Berman and David A. Lake (eds). *Proxy Wars: Suppressing Violence Through Local Agents.* Cornell University Press.
28 Berman et al. 2019.
29 Ibid.
30 For example, see Robert Axelrod (1984). *The Evolution of Cooperation.* Basic Books.
31 Berman et al. 2019.
32 Pettersson et al. 2021; Salehyan 2010.
33 Sabine C. Carey and Neil J. Mitchell (2017). "Progovernment Militias". *Annual Review of Political Science* 20: 127–47; Aliyev 2019.

34 Groh 2019, chapter 4; Reinoud Leenders and Antonio Giustozzi (2020). "Foreign Sponsorship of Progovernment Militias Fighting Syria's Insurgency: Whither Proxy Wars?". *Mediterranean Politics*. doi:10.1080/1362 9395.2020.1839235
35 Groh 2019, chapter 4; Leenders and Giustozzi 2020.
36 The logic here mirrors the reasoning of pushing states toward multilateral organizations. See Kenneth W. Abbott and Duncan Snidal (1998). "Why States Act Through Formal International Organizations". *Journal of Conflict Resolution* 42 (1): 3–32.
37 James D. Fearon (1994). "Domestic Political Audiences and the Escalation of International Disputes". *American Political Science Review* 88 (3): 577–92.
38 Bruce Bueno de Mesquita, Alastair Smith, Randolph M. Siverson, and James D. Morrow (2003). *The Logic of Political Survival*. MIT Press.
39 Mumford 2013; Groh 2019; Salehyan 2010; Moghadam and Wyss 2020.
40 Jessica L. Weeks (2008). "Autocratic Audience Costs: Regime Type and Signaling Resolve". *International Organization* 62 (1): 35–64.
41 Belgin San-Acka (2021). "The Role of Agency in the Formation of State-NAG Alliances" in Niklas Karlén et al. "Forum: Conflict delegation in Civil Wars". *International Studies Review* 23: 2048–78.
42 Krieg and Rickli 2019, chapter 1.
43 Belgin San-Acka (2016). *States in Disguise: Causes of State Support for Rebel Groups*. New York: Oxford University Press.
44 Fearon (2015) is the classic presentation of the bargaining framework for interstate war. Walter (2009) provides a thorough review of the application of the framework to intrastate conflict. See James D. Fearon (2015). "Rationalist Explanations of War". *International Organization* 49 (3): 379–414; Barbara F. Walter (2009). "Bargaining Failures and Civil War". *Annual Review of Political Science* 12: 243–61.
45 Kathleen Gallagher Cunningham (2013). "Actor Fragmentation and Civil War Bargaining: How Internal Divisions Generate Civil Conflict". *American Journal of Political Science* 57 (3): 659–72.
46 S. Carey, N. Mitchell, and W. Lowe (2013). "States, the Security Sector, and the Monopoly of Violence: A New Database on Pro-Government Militias". *Journal of Peace Research* 50 (2): 249–58.
47 J.A. Stanton (2015). "Regulating Militias: Governments, Militias, and Civilian Targeting in Civil War". *Journal of Conflict Resolution* 59 (5): 899–923.
48 Balch-Lindsay et al. 2000; Stephen E. Gent (2008). "Going in When It Counts: Military Intervention and the Outcome of Civil Conflicts". *International Studies Quarterly* 52 (4): 713–35; Patricia L. Sullivan and Johannes Karreth (2015). "The Conditional Impact of Military Intervention on Internal Armed Conflict Outcomes". *Conflict Management and Peace Science* 32 (3): 269–88; Reed M. Wood and Jacob D. Kathman (2014). "Too Much of a Bad Thing? Civilian Victimization and Bargaining in Civil War". *British Journal of Political Science* 44 (3): 685–706.
49 Sullivan and Karreth 2015.
50 Stathis N. Kalyvas (2006). *The Logic of Violence in Civil War*. New York: Cambridge University Press.

51 Grant and Kaussler 2020.
52 Mumford 2013; Ailyev 2019; Moghadam and Wyss 2020.
53 Leenders and Giustozzi 2020.
54 Groh 2019, chapters 1 and 2.
55 Kalyvas 2006.
56 Zeev and Belgin San-Akca (2012). "Rivalry and State Support of Non-State Armed Groups (NAGs), 1946–2001".
International Studies Quarterly 56 (4): 720–34; Emily Kalah Gade, Mohammed M. Hafez, and Michael Gabbay (2019). "Fratricide in Rebel Movements: A Network Analysis of Syrian Militant Infighting". *Journal of Peace Research* 56 (3): 321–35; Kristin M. Bakke, Kathleen Gallagher Cunningham, and Lee J. M. Seymour (2012). "A Plague of Initials: Fragmentation, Cohesion, and Infighting in Civil Wars". *Perspectives on Politics* 10 (2): 265–83.

3 Proxy War in the Middle East

This chapter provides an overview of how proxy warfare has become the dominant form of war in the Middle East since the invasion of Iraq by the United States in 2003. We argue that the invasion represented a systemic shock to the regional balance of power and ushered in over almost two decades of proxy war between regional powers, Western powers, and Russia. The Arab Spring revolution-turned civil wars in Syria and Libya are recognized as important theaters in this trajectory.

In 2019, the Uppsala Conflict Data Program listed ten active state-based conflicts in the Middle East.[1] Throughout that period and 2020, the wars in Libya, Iraq, Syria, and Yemen remained all internationalized conflicts where several regional and outside powers were either acting as external patrons to proxies or were active belligerents themselves. Regional security remained particularly susceptible to the geopolitical ambitions of regional powers such as Iran, Turkey, and Saudi Arabia nested within the more global ambitions of "super patrons" including the United States and Russia. The military intervention by Russia in 2015 on behalf of the Syrian regime effectively ensured the regime's survival and made the country a de facto Russian protectorate in 2017. The isolationist foreign policy of the Trump administration witnessed US troops withdrawing from positions in northern Syria in November 2019, which led to joint control of that part of Syria between Russian and Turkish forces.[2] The US "maximum pressure" campaign against Iran resulted in direct and indirect military escalation between both countries in the Persian Gulf. While the Middle East experienced the entire spectrum of violent conflict throughout its modern history ranging from civil war, state failure, outside invasion and occupation, nuclear proliferation, inter-state, ethnic and religious conflict, the 2003 invasion of Iraq ushered in a period during which war by proxy became the dominant form of warfare in the region. Notwithstanding his own government's tacit military support for the

DOI: 10.4324/9781003262602-3

Saudi war effort in Yemen,[3] the then British Foreign Secretary Boris Johnson reflected on this trend in 2016:

> There are politicians who are twisting and abusing religion and different strains of the same religion in order to further their own political objectives. That's one of the biggest political problems in the whole region. And the tragedy for me – and that's why you have these proxy wars being fought the whole time in that area – is that there is not strong enough leadership in the countries themselves ... That's why you've got the Saudis, Iran, everybody, moving in, and puppeteering and playing proxy wars.[4]

Likewise, all three US administrations since George W. Bush also staunchly underwrote the Saudi war effort in Yemen. By all accounts, it appeared that support for war by surrogate remained a dominant feature in the Middle East, used by both regional and outside powers.

Iraq

It was not until the invasion of Iraq in 2003 and what one US diplomat in Baghdad called the start of the "Great Game of Mesopotamia" in 2009 that war by proxy became the dominant form of interstate conflict in the Middle East. At the time, the US government was well aware that the Iraqi government viewed Iran as "posing risks" that were considered "manageable" rather than existential to its national interests. Sunni Arab states, however, feared that Iraq "would fall into Iran's orbit and rendered unable to speak of act independently". Fear in Riyadh and elsewhere was that once US forces withdrew from Iraq, the Iranians favored a government in Baghdad that would be "Shia-dominated", "weak and disenfranchised from its Arab neighbors, detached from US security apparatus and strategically dependent on Iran".[5] What the US Embassy in Baghdad labeled the "Great Game" related to concerted efforts by regional powers to intervene in Iraq intent to keep it weak.

Ultimately, the 2003 invasion and occupation of Iraq by US forces represented a systemic shock to Middle East security. The Bush administration had removed two of Iran's main rivals, Saddam Hussein in Iraq and the Taliban in Afghanistan, and helped create the first Shi'a Arab government in history. As Iraq's Sunnis were faced with the reality of being a demographic as well as political minority for the first time in the country's history, a highly devolved and weak central government in Baghdad never fully enjoyed monopoly of violence nor ever assumed the role as a neutral arbiter over the sectarian conflict that ensued. Eager to undercut the Shia-led Islamic Supreme Council of Iraq (ISCI) and Iraqi National Alliance (INA), the Saudi government subsequently used their money and media power to support Sunni political aspirations in the country. Likewise, Iran funded those and other Shi'a parties.[6] The neo-conservative vision of politically engineering a new benign Iraqi government post-Saddam Hussein ushered in a decade of political violence in the country. Iraq had become the region's center for terrorist groups, organized crime, and outside interference. As foreign and Iraqi militias and terrorist groups engaged in political violence that fueled the insurgency and slow-burning civil war, the central government itself found itself challenged by powerbrokers both from within Iraq's political spectrum and from across the region.

Libya

The Arab Spring uprisings in 2011 and subsequent descent into civil war in Libya and Syria would further draw in the Great Powers and regional rivals to intervene. Following the demise of the Qadhafi regime after NATO's 2011 military campaign and a series of failed UN attempts at post-conflict stabilization and political reconciliation, Libya split into two rival governments. Each government controlled their own territory and enjoyed backing from regional rivals. Turkey and Qatar supported military efforts by the internationally recognized government (Government of National Accord [GNA]) of Prime Minister Fayez al-Sarraj in Tripoli, while Egypt and the United Arab Republic backed the Libyan National Army (LNA) military forces led by General Khalifa Haftar who was allied with the rival government in the eastern part of Libya.[7] The UAE became one of Haftar's main supporters and, in violation of the UN arms embargo, supplied the LNA with advanced military equipment.[8] In fact, what took many observers by surprise was when in 2014, the UAE unilaterally launched air strikes inside Libya to help its proxies at tremendous distance without requesting or requiring US assistance.[9]

Russian mercenaries too joined Haftar forces and with the backing of Moscow made it increasingly difficult for the GNA to effectively check the general's political ambitions.[10] Haftar eventually tried to seize the capital but his forces were beaten back by Turkey-backed GNA forces. A subsequent stalemate eventually forced belligerents into negotiations leading to a UN-mediated political process, which called for a unity government and largely reduced violence by the end of 2021.[11]

Syria

Likewise in Syria, competitive external intervention by the Great Powers as well as regional rivals poured in enough resources for the conflict to defy any settlement, descent into total war, and cause the greatest refugee crisis for Europe since the end of World War II. With Iran, Saudi Arabia having demarcated the conflict along sectarian lines, jihadi groups, loyalists, and warlords operating in an emerging political economy of war, all were sustained by their respective external patrons. While Iranian-backed Iraqi Shi'a militias, Hezbollah, Revolutionary Guard commandos and Russian military forces would reinforce the embattled regime, Turkish, Saudi and Qatari supported opposition fighters. Not only did direct support to Syrian proxies prolong and harden the conflict, multilateral peace-making efforts were offset by US and European support for rebels and Chinese and Russian support for the regime.[12] By all accounts, Turkey was the most contradictory external disruptor in the Syrian theater. Even though a NATO member and close US ally, the Turkish policy under Recep Tayyip Erdogan was primarily driven by its shared borders with Syria and the influx of refugees into Turkey, and also by its intention to check the People's Protection Unit (YPG) which it considers a terrorist organization and linked to the outlawed Kurdish Workers Party PKK. However, the YPG also formed the main US proxy inside Syria in its fight against ISIS since 2015. As means to "voluntarily" resettle one million of the 3.7 million refugees residing in Turkey back into Syria, Turkish forces also took over large parts of the country through three major military operations.[13] Russian military intervention in Syria started in the fall of 2015 after an official request by the Assad regime. Ultimately, had it not been for Russian air supremacy and concerted air campaigns that targeted rebel-held territories, combined with Iranian-backed militias on the ground, the regime would not have reasserted control over most of the country. Russia's military campaign in Syria was brutal and its indiscriminate bombing of cities across the country costs the lives of countless of civilians. General Aleksandr Dvornikov, who was in charge of the campaign became known as the "butcher of Syria", was put in charge of Russian forces in Ukraine after Russia invaded its neighbor in 2022.[14] Russian military operations in Syria largely foreshadowed tactics which would then be used in occupied Ukraine. Much like in Ukraine, Russia deployed small units of Spetsnaz special forces onto frontlines across Syria where they partnered not with Syrian forces, but with better trained and experienced Lebanese Hezbollah. According to Russian military officer, when Spetsnaz troops returned from Syria, "some returned to Russia bearing tattoos of Shia iconography as a reminder of their Hezbollah "blood brothers".[15] Russia's campaign in Syria shifted the military balance in favor of Assad. Russia's ongoing presence in Syria largely is meant to make Syria a "sphere of influence" for Moscow. In line with the so-called Primakov doctrine, Russia attempts to counterbalance against a unipolar US-dominated world order. The Syrian intervention is a prime example of this Russian mindset.[16] Putin recognized that external actors were going to either control or influence large areas of Syria, including the United States, Russian intervention was largely meant to deny any one country to control the country. As Mona Yacobian puts it:

> bound by Syria's complex conflict dynamics, Moscow's strategy acquiesces to Syria's de facto zones of control that essentially translate into three major spheres of influence: Russia in the west, particularly along Syria's strategic spine; Turkey in the north; and begrudgingly for Moscow, the United States in the east.[17]

Reminiscent of 19th-century Great Power politics, Syria had essentially been carved into opposing spheres of influences by outsider powers. It is a situation where US, Turkish, and Russian forces largely avoid direct confrontations. By 2022, there were less than 1,000 US forces in the country with the mandate of engaging against ISIS, while approximately 4000 Russian forces with heavy military equipment conduced operations in support of the regime. The Turkish military mainly relied on proxies to regain control of territories in the north while Iran and Israel were locked in a fight in which Israel conduced air attacks against Iranian proxies (mainly Hezbollah) and to disrupt weapon shipments into Syria.[18] With ISIS largely defeated, by 2022, the Syrian political-military map remained entirely dominated by external actors: US-supported Kurdish forces, Russian- and Iranian-backed regime units, and Turkish forces backed by Syrian proxies.[19]

Yemen

When the Houthi rebel forces deposed the government in Yemen and took over the capital in 2015, the ensuing civil war in the country would become the latest proxy war theater in the region. While Saudi Arabia largely framed these new realities along national security considerations given its extensive border and history with its southern neighbor, Iran saw the turmoil inside Yemen as opportunity to help a

Shi'a aligned group become the dominant political force and ultimately use a Houthi-led Yemen and the war itself as means to check against Saudi power. Iranian leaders were less invested in the political future of Yemen than their Saudi counterparts. While they certainly favor a Houthi-run government, the immediate objective was to bait and bleed Saudi Arabia into a lengthy war. The ideological make-up of Houthis, the history of Saudi interventions inside Yemen and Iran's quick pace to provide them with funds and political-military support represented an instant formula for proxy war.

Houthis belong to the Shi'a sect known as Zaydi named after Zayd bin Ali bin Hussein (the great grandson of the Prophet Muhammad) who fought against the Umayyad Caliphate was killed in the battle at Kufa in 740. However, unlike the Twelver Shi'a, Zaydi believe that the leadership assed to Zayd and not his brother—Muhammad al-Baqir, the Twelver's fifth Iman—after the death of their father, Ali bin Hussein.[20] Zaydi eventually established themselves in the northern mountainous region of Yemen and for the next thousand years would attempt to rule over the country. They fought against both the Ottomans and Wahhabis in the 18th and 19th centuries and ruled part of Yemen until a republican coup in 1962 overthrew their last Imam.[21] More than just causing political violence and turmoil in the country, the military coup also heralded a military intervention by Egypt under Gamal Abdul Nasser. What became known as "Nasser's Vietnam" was a lengthy and destructive military intervention that started with three Egyptian brigades in 1962 and increased to four divisions by 1965. Egyptian decision-makers knew nothing about Yemen's social structures or politics. As Egyptian forces found themselves fighting Zaydi insurgents in mountainous terrain, Nasser later himself reflected on his decision being a "miscalculation; we never thought that it would lead to what it did."[22] It was the Middle East's first proxy war during the Cold War. Nasser's intervention would put Egypt and the Soviet Union against Saudi Arabia, Britain, the United States, and Israel who were supporting Yemen's royalists. While republican forces ultimately won the civil war and Saudi Arabia recognized the new republic in North Yemen in a peace agreement in 1970, Egyptian forces had largely withdrawn by 1967, leaving Nasser deprived of US aid and more indebted to the Kremlin for military assistance.[23] Despite heavy Soviet influence in Iraq, Syria, and Egypt, South Yemen became the People's Democratic Republic of Yemen in 1969 and the only truly socialist government in the Middle East during the Cold War. North and South Yemen had two brief wars in 1972 and 1979 with the North being supplied by Saudi Arabia and the South by the USSR. Both conflicts demonstrated the strength of the People's Republic's military power and both ended with formal agreements for unifications between both states.²⁴ Saudi Arabia played a vital role in both initially exacerbating North-side enmity and then helping them move toward reunification. In the early days of North and South Yemen, Saudi rulers were wary of any potential challenging ideological forces from either government and strongly supported monarchist forces in both countries. Saudi evenhandedness changed after the South Yemen formed an alliance with the USSR in the mid-1970s. Riyadh started to support North Yemen militarily as well as provided support to rebel forces in the South. Saudi policy toward Yemen's reunification changed as relations between the South and Riyadh improved as Saudi rulers reduced its military aid to the North. Seeking a balance between the North and South, Saudi Arabia was actively mediating cease-fire talks and eventually supported the re-unification of the country.²⁵

Houthis themselves emerged in the early 1990s as an opposition movement to the government and actually prefer the name Ansar Allah ("Partisans of God"). Named after Hussein Badr al-Din al-Huthi, the movement was essentially a Zaydi revivalist movement protesting the economic, political, and cultural marinization of their region as well as countering Wahhabi influence in schools in the north.²⁶ Again, Saudi influence in Yemen would play an important factor in shaping Yemeni politics. The Houthis' armed rebellion against the government in 2004 led to a protracted insurgency against President Ali Abdullah Saleh. During a total of six major military campaigns or the so-called "Sa'dah wars" between 2004 and 2009, Houthi rebels were fighting against nearly every of the government's military and security branches, none of which, however, were able to quell the insurgency. By 2009, 250,000 people were internally displaced in Sa'dah, Amran, Hajja and Sana'a and the conflict had already started to have a devastating impact on the economy.²⁷ During the insurgency period, Houthis earned their battle stripes and built a military organization, while the Yemeni government seemed unable to check the group's rise. It was during this period that both Saudi Arabia and Iran started to intervene. Initially, Saudi Arabia had started allowing Yemeni government forces into its territory to attack Houthis from the north. In retaliation, Houthis launched incursions into Saudi Arabia which prompted Riyadh to launch air strikes against Houthi positions.²⁸ The measures seemed to have caused Iran to step up its patronage role over Houthis. According to a 2015 report to the UN Security Council's Iran Sanctions Committee, Iran probably started providing small amounts of weapons to the Houthis during this period (2009).[29] It is important to emphasize that the ruling cadre, the "Sa'dah Core" who survived the "Sa'dah wars" not only advanced to nationwide leadership of the group but also is that subset of Houthis whose ideologies lean closest to Iran's Twelver Shi'ism. Many Shi'a customs and celebrations that were non-existent in Yemen prior to the war were being incorporated. For example, the commemoration of Ashura was publicly celebrated by Houhtis supporters for the first time in 2017 and Shi'as across the country now also observe Eid al-Ghadr, a celebration which previously was allegedly only held in secret. It is not surprising therefore that the so-called "Sa'dah Core" is the faction that has the closest ties to Iran's IRGC and Lebanon's Hezbollah advising Houthi leadership.[30]

Ignoring Saudi pleas not to remove Saddam Hussein from power in 2003, the Bush administration's invasion of Iraq caused a systemic shock to the region that not only had destroyed the existing order (which was largely based on US-extended deterrence) but also opened the doors for regional powers to compete for regional dominance. The neo-conservative objective to politically engineer new Middle Eastern democracies that would help the United States to projects its power across the region failed. The United States showed that it had power to destroy a regime and its armed forces, but lengthy and costly nation-building came at price politically. While Obama had to increase troops to both Afghanistan and Iraq during his tenure even though he had vowed to bring US forces back home, a new US "offshore mentality" already came of age during his White House years. Especially after the killing of Bin Laden, neither Red nor Blue America was willing to support any more US military interventions in the Middle East or anywhere else overseas. So, while proxy war became the warfare of choice for regional powers as they found themselves locked in conflicts beset on baiting and bleeding their opponent, successive US presidents after George W. Bush opted to act as a patron to local surrogates not because it was the strategically the best option but because it was the only one politically. All of this meant that the Middle East found itself locked in the most destructive period in its modern history. War had become permanent and almost every Middle Eastern country was involved in some sort of open or covert military campaign.

In Yemen, the formula for proxy war was effectively built into the political and ideological makeup of the country. It was unacceptable to the Saudi leadership that a group who was benign to Iran would be permitted to govern Yemen. Even if Iran did not intend to bait Saudi Arabia into a prolonged and destructive war, it used its patronage over Houthis effectively to that end. Finally, Yemen was featured prominently in US national security thinking because of the presence of al-Qaeda and other radical Islamists groups and because Iran further expanding its threat network with the help of another Shi'a militia group was seen as an unacceptable scenario for any of the three presidents in the White House during this period. It is important to emphasize that Houthis considered any US counter terrorism raid as "state terrorism".[31]

After 2015, Yemen found itself yet again as pawn of regional and great power rivalry. As external patrons entered the conflict in Yemen, we can identify their respective perceptions, motivations, and objectives as follows:

1   A Houthi-run government in Yemen was unacceptable to Saudi Arabia. When Saudi rulers formed a coalition and launched the intervention in 2015 their objective was to destroy the Houthi movement and reinstall the Hadi government. As Saudi Arabia supported Yemeni government forces in their fight against Houthis, it also established a blockade on Yemen which prevented humanitarian aid from being delivered at all of the country's air, land and sea ports. While Saudi and UAE ground forces were fighting on the ground, we argue that Saudi and coalition air attacks against targets in Yemen would prove to be the conflict's most destructive feature. Not only was Saudi Arabia an active belligerent in the conflict, it also acted as a proxy to the United States as well as a patron to the Hadi government. Saudi objectives were maximalist in that they sought the reinstatement of the Hadi government who ruled from exile in Riyadh since 2015. Seen by most Yemenis as a Saudi puppet, the Hadi government became a Saudi proxy and was closely tied to both Saudi interests and demands.

2   The Iranian government entered the war on the side of the Houthis. Identifying the Houthis as another group in what the US military calls "Iran Threat Network"[32] and what Iran would see as the "axis of resistance" against the United States and its regional allies, the Iranian government primarily entered the war in order to "bait and bleed" Saudi resources. Support for Houthis was meant to balance against Saudi Arabia rather than politically engineer a Houthi government, though it would certainly favor such an outcome. Unlike Saudi Arabia, Iran entered the war covertly. Throughout the conflict, Iran denied sending weapons but rather just publicly supported Houthis as the legitimate government for Yemen. Unlike, Saudi Arabia, Iran also had no direct political objectives for Yemen and on numerous occasions

called for a political dialogue between the belligerents. Supporting Houthis with resources was sufficient for decision-makers in Iran as this strategy helped shift the balance of power to the Houthi's favor and drained Saudi resources making them ultimately look weak. To Tehran, prolonging the war without attempting to impose any particular political framework on Yemen was an end in itself. While Houthis were technically Iran's proxies in their geopolitical strife against Saudi Arabia, Houthis enjoyed a good amount of autonomy in both decision-making and dependency. While they did rely on Iranian military support, the relationship between Houthis and Iran was somewhat more equal than between Saudi Arabia and the Hadi government. Houthis were seen as means to balance against Saudi Arabia. As far as Houthis were concerned, Iran was perceived as an ally rather than domineering patron. In fact, had it not been for Saudi Arabia's intervention, it is unlikely that Iran would have entered the war as an external patron in the first place.

3   While Saudi Arabia's military intervention caused Iran to support Houthis, Iranian involvement in Yemen ultimately triggered US involvement in the war. We use the term "super patron" to describe the role of the United States in the conflict as it used Saudi Arabia (who itself was an external patron as well as active belligerent) as means to balance against Iran. Three US presidents, Barrack Obama, Donald Trump, and Joe Biden largely framed the conflict along a realist mindset. Beyond targeting AQAP and later ISIS inside Yemen with US special forces and UAV's, none of the administrations had any clear interest in Yemen's political future. The wars in Iraq and Afghanistan had tempered any interest in nation building in the Middle East. Largely, all three successive administrations embraced an "offshore mentality" toward the country and used Saudi military power to contain Iran. Much like Reagan's policy of "no losers and no winners" during the Iran-Iraq war when the United States supported Saddam Hussein's regime to offshore balance against Iran, US policy toward Yemen was intended to defeat another manifestation of Iran's threat network. With Iranian proxies already operating in Lebanon, Iraq, and Syria, US military support for Saudi Arabia was meant to disrupt and destroy Iran's infrastructure in the country. While the United States would support the UN framework for negotiating peace, all three administrations (in particular the Obama and Trump administrations) had no direct political objectives for Yemen. The lessons from Iraq, Libya, and Afghanistan dictated this new US "offshore

mentality", which prevented presidents from engaging in any more political engineering but rather opted to support Saudi Arabia as a proxy against Iran. As Acting US Assistant Secretary for State, David M. Satterfield stated in 2018: "U.S. military support for the Saudi-led coalition in Yemen serves a clear purpose—to reinforce Saudi and Emirati action on behalf of the Yemeni government in the face of intensified Houthi threats and to expand the capability of our Gulf partners to push back themselves against Iran's destabilizing actions."[33] As the only democracy in the conflict, we also argue that the United States was also the most susceptible to public opinion about the nature of the war and civilian deaths.

We identify following groups and militaries as the most important actors in the conflict:

- **Republic of Yemen Government (ROYG):** The internationally recognized government of Yemen, with a temporary capital in Aden city. Abd-Rabbu Mansour Hadi was the President of Yemen from 2012 through April, 2022 when he ceded power to the Presidential Leadership Council. He governed in exile from Riyadh since the Houthi. The government controls 40,000 forces including militias.
- **Houthi forces:** Houthis themselves prefer the name "Ansar Allah" (Champions of God). There are about 20,000 Houthis forces in Yemen.[34]
- **Saudi-Led Coalition (SLC):** Military coalition of nine countries led by Saudi Arabia to support the ROYG. Member countries include United Arab Emirates, Kuwait, Qatar (until 2017), Egypt, Morocco, Jordan, Sudan, and Bahrain. As of 2022, under Operation "Restoring Hope", there are 2,500 Saudi forces and 650 Sudanese forces in Yemen.
- **United Arab Emirates (UAE):** The UAE has been part of the SLC from the onset and deployed approximately 3,500 ground forces in Yemen and another 3,000 additional airmen, sailors, and soldiers operating in direct support offshore and in neighboring regions. The UAE withdrew most of their forces from Yemen in 2019.[35]
- **Iran's Islamic Revolutionary Guard Corps Quds Force (IRGC):** The number of IRGC special forces in Yemen is unknown. The IRGC act as the main liaison between Iran and Houthis as well as coordinated, trained, and supplied them with weapons ranging from smalls arms to UAV's and long range missiles.[36]

- **Southern Transitional Council (STC):** It is a UAE-supported southern secessionist group formed by dismissed Aden Governor'Aidarous al-Zubaydi in May 2017.[37]
- **Al-Qa'ida in the Arabian Peninsula (AQAP):** It is currently known as Ansar al-Shari'ah, founded in 2009 when the Yemeni and Saudi branches of al-Qa'ida merged, with active strongholds in southern Yemen.
- **US military:** By 2022, the United States still maintained 2,120 forces in Saudi Arabia in order to "protect United States forces and interests in the region against hostile action by Iran and Iran-backed groups" and small number of special forces in Yemen to "conduct operations against al-Qaeda in the Arabian Peninsula and ISIS".[38] In 2022, there were 120 military advisers working in Saudi Arabia for the US Military Training Mission.[39]
- **Popular Resistance (PR):** A conglomerate of pro-ROYG and anti-Houthi tribal forces with varied motivations; the term Popular Resistance is used broadly in the media and can also encompasses the Southern Resistance.

Notes

1 Uppsala Conflict Data Program, "UCDP GED Map: Active State-Based Conflicts in 2019", https://ucdp.uu.se/downloads/charts/#__utma=1.486322752.1605624777.1605624777.1605624777.1&__utmb=1.6.10.1605624777&__utmc=1&__utmx=-&__utmz=1.1605624777.1.1.utmcsr=google|utmccn=(organic)|utmcmd=organic|utmctr=(not%20provided)&__utmv=-&__utmk=97288863 (accessed 12 November 2020).
2 "Chapter Seven: Middle East and North Africa" (2020), *The Military Balance* 120 (1): 324–87.
3 By 2019, it was revealed that British technicians working for British defense contractors were working on Saudi air force bases and, according to a BAE Systems staff, constituted a major asset without which the Saudi air campaign against Yemen could not be maintained. The British and US military also had liaisons in the Saudi Air Operations Center in Riyadh, see Channel 4 News (1 April 2019). "Britain's Hidden War: Channel 4 Dispatches", https://www.channel4.com/press/news/britains-hidden-war-channel-4-dispatches (accessed 11 December 2020).
4 Vladimir Rauta (2020). "Proxy Warfare and the Future of Conflict: Take Two". *The RUSI Journal* 165 (2): 38.
5 Alexander Star (2011). *Open Secrets: WikiLeaks, War and American Diplomacy*. Grove Press, pp. 74–8, 293–99.
6 Ibid.
7 Robert Malley, "10 Conflicts to Watch for in 2020". *Foreign Policy* (26 December 2019), https://foreignpolicy.com/2019/12/26/10-conflicts-to-watch-2020/ (accessed 20 March 2021).

8 See UN Security Council, Letter dated 29 November 2019 from the Panel of Experts on Libya established pursuant to resolution 1973 (2011) addressed to the President of the Security Council, S/2019/914 (9 December 2019), p. 66, 73, 88–9, 125–6, 191–5, 221–2, 255–93.
9 David B. Roberts (2021). "Lifting the Protection Curse: The Rise of New Military Powers in the Middle East". *Survival* 63 (2), https://www.tandfonline.com/doi/full/10.1080/00396338.2021.1905997
10 In defiance of UN-brokered agreement, Russian-backed mercenaries did not withdraw from Libya but rather had built a 43-mile-long trench and military fortifications in January 2021. Nick Paton Walsh and Sarah el-Sirgany, "Foreign Fighters Were Meant to Leave Libya This Week. A Huge Trench Being Dug by Russian-Backed Mercenaries Indicates They Plan to Stay". *CNN* (22 January 2021), https://www.cnn.com/2021/01/22/africa/libya-trench-russia-intl/index.html
11 "Chapter Seven: The Middle East and North Africa". The Military Balance, 122 (1): 321.
12 Raymond Hinnebusch and Adham Saouli (2020). *The War for Syria: Regional and International Dimensions of the Syrian Uprising*. Routledge, pp. 1–17.
13 Bassem Mroue and Zeynep Bilginsoy, "Explainers: What's behind Turkey's Syria Incursion Threats". The Associated Press (3 June 2022), https://apnews.com/article/russia-ukraine-islamic-state-group-politics-middle-east-a1293989c40712ae4a789311f88bcb45
14 Charles Lister, "What's Putin's Next Move? Look to Syria". *Politico* (27 March 2022), https://www.politico.com/news/magazine/2022/04/27/russia-putin-next-move-syria-00028041 (accessed 12 June 2022).
15 Ibid.
16 Moca Yacobian,"What's Russia's Endgame for Syria? US Institute for Peace" (16 February 12021), https://www.usip.org/publications/2021/02/what-russias-endgame-syria (accessed 12 June 2022).
17 Ibid.
18 The Military Balance 2022, p. 321.
19 Ibid.
20 Hamad H. Albboshi (2016). "Ideological Roots of the Huthi Movement in Yemen". *Journal of Arabian Studies* 6 (2): 144–5.
21 Ibid; Thomas Juneau (2021). "How War in Yemen Transformed the Iran-Houthi Partnership, Studies in Conflict and Terrorism", https://www.tandfonline.com/doi/full/10.1080/1057610X.2021.1954353; Bruce Riedel, "Who Are the Houthis and Why Are We at War with Them?". *Brookings* (18 December 2017), https://www.brookings.edu/blog/markaz/2017/12/18/who-are-the-houthis-and-why-are-we-at-war-with-them/ (accessed 14 June 2022).
22 A.I. Dawisha (1975). "Intervention in the Yemen: An Analysis of Egyptian Perceptions and Policies". *Middle East Journal* 29 (1): 48; Thanos Petouris (2015). Jesse Ferris. "Nasser's Gamble: How Intervention in Yemen Caused the Six-Day War and the Decline of Egyptian Power"; Aaron Edwards. "Mad Mitch's Tribal Law: Aden and the End of Empire". *Asian Affairs* 46 (2): 327.
23 Thanos Petouris (2015) Jesse Ferris. "Nasser's Gamble: How Intervention in Yemen Caused the Six-Day War and the Decline of Egyptian Power; Aaron Edwards. Mad Mitch's Tribal Law: Aden and the End of Empire";

Jude Kadri (2021). "Impact of 1962-68 North Yemen War on Cold War Balance of Power". *Middle East Critique* 30 (3): 265–86.
24 Helen Lackner (2017). "The People's Democratic Republic of Yemen: Unique Socialist Experiment in the Arab World at Time of Revolutionary Fervor". *Interventions* 19: 682.
25 Lu XIA (2010). "Regional Factors in Yemen's Integration Reunification". *Journal of Middle Eastern and Islamic Studies* (in Asia) 4 (4): 112.
26 Thomas Juneau, How War in Yemen transformed the Iran-Houthi Partnership, Studies in Conflict and Terrorism (2021), p. 3.
27 Christopher Boucek, "War in Saada: From Local Insurrection to National Challenge". A Carnegie Paper Series No. 110 (April 2010), https://carnegieendowment.org/files/war_in_saada.pdf (accessed 11 June 2022).
28 Thomas Juneau (2021). How War in Yemen Transformed the Iran-Houthi Partnership, Studies in Conflict and Terrorism.
29 Ibid.
30 Sama'a al-Hamdani, "Understanding the Houthi Faction in Yemen". *Lawfare Blog* (17 April 2019), https://www.lawfareblog.com/understanding-houthi-faction-yemen (accessed 9 June 2022).
31 US Department of State, "Yemen Situation Report" (30 January 2017), https://foia.state.gov/Search/Results.aspx?searchText=Yemen&beginDate=20150101&endDate=20220622&publishedBeginDate=&publishedEndDate=&caseNumber= (accessed 9 June 2022).
32 See Michael Knights, Crispin Smith, and Hamdi Malik, "Discordance in the Iran Threat Network in Iraq: Militia Competition and Rivalry", 14 (8), West Point – Combating Terrorism Center (October 2021), https://ctc.westpoint.edu/discordance-in-the-iran-threat-network-in-iraq-militia-competition-and-rivalry/ (accessed 20 June 2022).
33 US Department of State, US Policy Toward a Turbulent Middle East (18 April 2018), House of Representatives, Committee on Foreign Affairs, https://foia.state.gov/Search/Results.aspx?searchText=(Yemen)%20AND%20(Yemen)&beginDate=20150101&endDate=20220622 (accessed 8 June 2022).
34 The Military Balance 2022, p. 377.
35 Michael Knights, "Lessons from the UAE War in Yemen". *Lawfare Blog* (18 August 2019), https://www.lawfareblog.com/lessons-uae-war-yemen (accessed 18 June 2022).
36 The Military Balance 2022, p. 340.
37 Navanti, Yemen: Incident Tracker (7–13 December 2020), 12; The Military Balance 2022, p. 377; Congressional Research Service, Congress and the War in Yemen: Oversight and Legislation 2015–2021 (updated 10 February 2022), https://sgp.fas.org/crs/mideast/R45046.pdf (accessed 20 June 2022).
38 The White House, "Letter to the Speaker of the House and President Pro Tempore of the Senate Regarding the War Powers Report" (7 December 2021), https://www.whitehouse.gov/briefing-room/statements-releases/2021/12/07/letter-to-the-speaker-of-the-house-and-president-pro-tempore-of-the-senate-regarding-the-war-powers-report-2/ (accessed 20 June 2022).
39 US Government Accountability Office, The Department of Defense (DOD) administered at least $54.6 billion of military support to Saudi Arabia and the United Arab Emirates (UAE) from fiscal years 2015 through 2021 (June 2022), https://www.gao.gov/assets/gao-22-105988.pdf (accessed 1 August 2022).

4 Key Military Engagements in Yemen, 2014–2022

In September 2014, Houthi rebels seized control of Yemen's capital city, Sana'a, marking the start of the civil war in Yemen. After failed attempts find a negotiated settlement and avoid war, Yemeni President Abd-Rabbu Mansour Hadi resigned as president in January 2015, fled Sana'a, rescinded his resignation, and requested intervention from neighboring Saudi Arabia to restore his government. Saudi Arabia responded by launching Operation Decisive Storm in March 2015, which saw the Saudis lead ten state coalition that included the United Arab Emirates, Bahrain, Kuwait, Egypt, Jordan, Morocco, Sudan, and Qatar in opposition to the Houthi rebel forces. From its inception, the civil war in Yemen was internationalized and reflected an expansive set of external interests in addition to the domestic question of governmental control. The Saudi-led coalition's intervention was the initial overt external involvement in what would become a seven-year civil war, but it was hardly the first external geostrategic interest that shaped the war.

Beginning with the Arab Spring in 2011, the Iranian government created the "iron fist" narrative of Saudi regional interventions in an effort to crush the Arab revolutions.[1] The Iranian government framed the Houthi takeover as a peoples' movement and called on the United States and Saudi Arabia to respect the political demands of the majority of Yemenis,[2] describing Saudi policies toward Yemen as "imperialist" in contrast to Iran's support for the "downtrodden people of Yemen".[3] Iranian clerics and government officials started a concerted campaign to frame Saudi Arabia as the aggressor following the commencement of Operation Decisive Storm in March 2015. For example, Ayatollah Lotfollah Safi-Golpayegani urged the Iranian Foreign Ministry to "use strong diplomacy" and "cut the oppressor's hand".[4] From the start, Saudi Arabia had claimed that Iranian military was supplying the Houthis with weaponry. Iran denied these charges, stating that its official position was to support an independent Yemeni state and oppose

DOI: 10.4324/9781003262602-4

"Saudi military aggression".[5] The Iranian government stuck to this narrative throughout the conflict, relying instead on symbolic or covert support for Houthis as to cast Saudi Arabia and the Gulf monarchies as the aggressors at the United Nation and in official statements while giving itself the veneer of speaking on behalf oppressed Yemenis. Iran was fighting in the shadows by proxy while Saudi Arabia and, by extension the United States as its underwriting super patron, found themselves on the defensive. While the Saudis scrambled to rebut allegations of civilian victimizations, war crimes, and the reckless behavior of intervening parties, Iran framed its own policy around providing humanitarian aid to Yemen, further constructing itself as a benevolent seeking to reduce the human impacts of the Saudi aggression.[6]

The Battle of Aden and the Onset of the War

Following the Houthis takeover and consolidation of Sana'a by late 2014, President Abd-Rabbu Mansour Hadi's government resigned in January 2015 and retreated to Aden. By March 2015, Houthis and forces loyal to former president Ali Abdullah Saleh advanced toward Aden, which at the time was the last stronghold of loyalists of Hadi regime.[7] In late March, Houthi forces captured the international airport in Aden, triggering the Saudi-led intervention, Operation Decisive Storm. Depicting Iran as the mastermind behind the scenes of the Houthi advance, the Saudi Ambassador to the United States described the conflict in Yemen as "a battle between good and evil".[8] Furthermore, in the eyes of Saudi decision-makers, the Houthis were Iranian proxies, meaning the fall of Aden was a prelude to the violent takeover of Yemen by Iran. In order to prevent this outcome and restore the legitimate government, direct intervention was required.[9]

Operation Decisive Strom began on 26 March with initial objectives of destroying ballistic missiles, aircrafts, and other heavy weapons that had been acquired by Houthi forces. During this month-long campaign, the coalition would launch 30 air strikes against targets in the Aden Governorate while local pro-Hadi forces fought on the ground against the Houthi rebels, transforming Aden into the first major battlefield of war. The Decisive Storm phase of the conflict was declared over on 22 April by Saudi Defense Minister Mohammed bin Salman, though the ground fighting and air campaign would continue. Figure 4.1 shows the evolution of ground and air campaigns in the Aden Governorate throughout 2015 according to the Armed Conflict Location and Events Data Project (ACLED).[10] The data present weekly aggregates of distinct battle and air strike events occurring

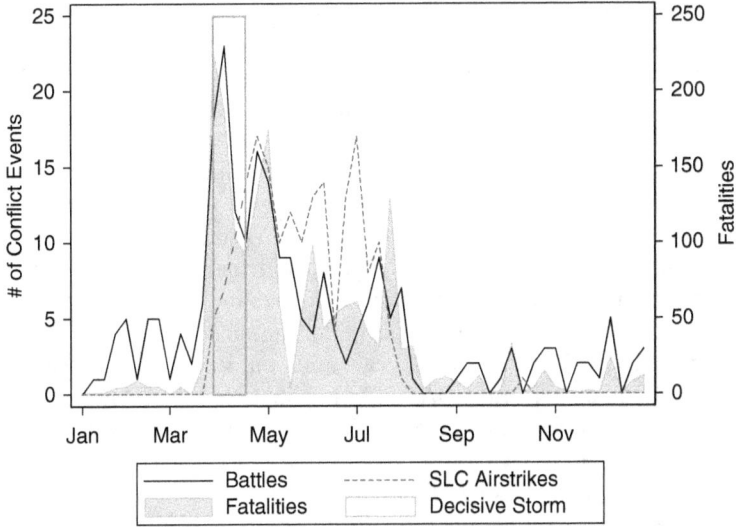

Figure 4.1 The Battle of Aden, 2015.

within the Aden Governorate as recorded by ACLED.[11] The data generally fit the Saudi narrative. The aerial campaign begins as a response to the rapid expansion of on-the-ground fighting as the Houthi approach the city of Aden and does correspond with a general reduction in the frequency of battles between Houthi and pro-regime forces. However, the aerial campaign continues at the same general intensity throughout August despite the Saudi claims of the operation's success and conclusion in April.

To many in Aden, this new conflict was reminiscent of the previous civil war and Houthis were perceived by locals as the latest northern invaders seeking to dominate the south, revealing additional domestic fault lines that would further complicate the emerging war.[12] As Hadi loyalists left Aden, local residents formed their own units and took to the streets to repel the advance of Houthis and their allied groups. Casualties rapidly expanded (Figure 4.1) prompting the UN Security Council to pass Resolution 2216 on April 14, 2015 demanding that Houthi forces "immediately and unconditionally end violence, withdraw forces from areas they have seized, relinquish all arms, cease activities undermining the authority of the country's legitimate Government, refrain from provocation against neighboring States, release the Defense Minister, and end the recruitment of children".[13] Instead, the conflict would expand.

The expanding conflict created opportunities for extremist groups such as Al Qaeda in the Arabian Peninsula to operate unfettered in Yemen. In Mukalla, Yemen's fifth largest city and the capital of the Hadramawt Governorate, Al-Qaeda in the Arabian Peninsula (AQAP) commandos broke into the prison and freed over 300 prisoners including AQAP leaders. They also attacked the governorate's headquarters, seizing the presidential palace, the central bank, the main police station, the coast guard building, the General People's Congress (GPC) headwaters, the Federation of Yemeni Women, and established checkpoints at all entrances to the city. Local tribal and governmental forces were unable to mount any meaningful counter-attacks, leading to Mukalla becoming an AQAP stronghold enabling operations across the region throughout the next year until an Emirati-led offensive recaptured Mukalla from AQAP. During that time, AQAP saw approximately $2 million in estimated daily revenue from customs fees levied on goods and fuel entering the port.[14]

In May 2015, Houthi forces fired mortar shells and rockets at targets inside Saudi territory, killing five Saudi citizens. These attacks triggered retaliatory attacks by the coalition, including more than 30 air raids and artillery attacks that reportedly killed 43 civilians in Yemen's Saada province.[15] This initial attack and the ensuing retaliation marked the start of the Houthi-Saudi border conflict. Figure 4.2 depicts the monthly

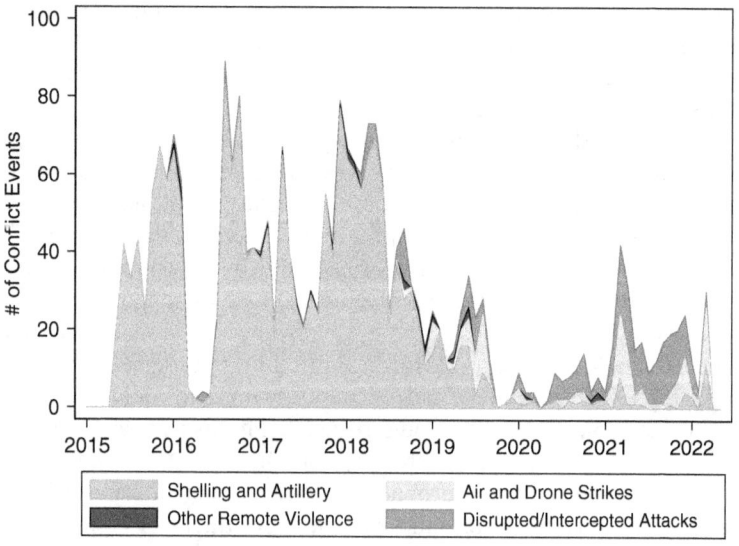

Figure 4.2 Houthi Remote Violence Against Targets Within Saudi Arabia.

progression of Houthi remote violence against targets inside Saudi Arabia as reported by ACLED.[16] Between 2015 and 2021, Houthi forces launched a series of ballistic missiles and artillery against Saudi targets; later in the conflict, as Iran's support for the Houthi movement became more overt, the Houthi would gain access to drones. Most targets were relatively close to the Yemeni border, however, some reached as far as north as the Saudi capital, Riyadh. Incoming missiles were frequently intercepted by Saudi air-defense systems, although many Saudi civilians were killed or wounded by shrapnel.[17] Despite the loss of civilian life, it would be successful strikes against Saudi oil refineries, the kingdom's most important infrastructure, that would made Saudi leadership look vulnerable to the Houthis and by extension Iran. For its part, the Iranian leadership continued to decry Saudi and coalition attacks on civilian targets in Yemen while aiding the Houthis in doing the same within Saudi territory.

As coalition forces attempted to retake Aden from Houthi control, UAE, Saudi Arabia, and Bahrain incurred their first heavy losses of the conflict. By the end of September, the Saudi offensive had claimed the lives of two high-ranking officers including Brigadier General Ibrahim Hamzi, deputy commander of the eighth brigade in Jazan.[18] Coalition forces retook control of Aden in July 2015. Saudi Arabia had covertly trained some 600 Yemeni fighters who joined with local militias that were already fighting Houthis in Aden. Provisioned with armored personnel carriers from Saudi Arabia, they were able to regain control of the airport, port, and most city neighborhoods.[19] The recapturing of Aden prompted exiled President Hadi and several of his ministers to return to Aden in September after six months in exile in Saudi Arabia with intentions to liberate the rest of the country.[20] However, beneath the much-publicized return of President Hadi was the reality that Saudi Arabia was clearly functioning as an external patron over Yemen, exerting power and control over the Yemeni government so much so that the legitimacy of the latter came into question. Notwithstanding that the government was supposed to be running the country from Aden, President Hadi only managed to stay one week before needing to return to Saudi Arabia. He would return to Aden for a second time in November 2016, though he only stayed a few days. He would only return to Aden once more in June 2018 before increasing fissures between the UAE leadership and the Yemeni government prevented the president from returning to the city. Aden remained under the de facto control of UAE-backed militias and the secessionist Southern Transitional Council (STC) that sought and independent southern Yemen. The government did not lose full control of Aden until the fall of 2019 when Foreign Minister Ahmed Almaisry had a falling out with the Emirati leadership and was forced to flee the country.[21] Thus, the recapturing of Aden marked an important milestone and a tactical victory for the coalition, but the subsequent tensions between the outside patron and the government revealed the limits of governing during proxy war.

The Houhti-Saleh Split

The Houithi-led protests that swept across Yemen in 2011, eventually leading to President Saleh's resignation in Saudi Arabia, signified a new era in Yemeni politics. When Houthi forces marched on Sana'a in 2014, the deposed president saw an opportunity to enact revenge on those who had forced him from office and a possible path back to power. Saleh still had significant influence and connections within the military and the northern tribal confederations, and agreed to an alliance with the Houthi that would provide them with access to weaponry and military equipment, unfettered passage, and access to smuggling lines crucial to Houthi readiness in the yearly conflict, and assistance from significant segments of the Yemeni Armed Forces that remained loyal to Saleh. At Saleh's behest, pro-Saleh factions of the Yemeni military stood down as Houthi forces entered and captured Sana'a in 2014; in some instances, they intervened to prevent pro-regime units from defending the city from the Houthi assault. After capturing the capital in September 2014, Houthi forces would retain control of the capital city throughout the war.

In August 2016, the Houthis together with Saleh's GPC transferred power from the Revolutionary Council to the newly formed Supreme Political Council (SPC) with top governmental positions to be eventually split between Houthi and GPC officials. The move was immediately rejected by the Saudi government and other than Iran, not a single country would recognize the council as the legitimate government of Yemen.[22] The composition of the SPC became a point of contention between the Houthi and GPC, with the former reluctant to truly share power. The Houthis intended to further sideline Saleh with a largely ceremonial position. While part of the council, Saleh was unwilling to further yield power. Tensions between Houthis and Saleh's supporters continued to rise throughout 2017, culminating when Saleh and the GPC staged a mass rally in the capital on August 24, 2017 to celebrate the 35th anniversary of the founding of the GPC only days after Houthis had called for declaring a state of emergency and a "suspension of all party activity" in the country.[23] Standing before a crowd of over 300,000 supporters, Saleh declared that "we are ready to flood the front lines not by the hundreds or thousands, but by the tens of thousands of fighters who are at home ... and the only thing the Houthi government has to do is to pay the salaries because we have the weapons".[24] Two days later, tensions between both factions would turn violent. Fighting erupted between members of the presidential guard and Houthi forces shortly after the rally. Although the former presidential palace where Saleh and his family resided had constituted a de facto no-go area for the Houthis to this point, Houthi forces attempted to establish a security checkpoint near the home of Saleh's son. Two people were killed, one of which was a senior aide to Saleh.[25]

The underlying political fissures between Saleh and the Houthis continued to escalate until the former president, in a televised address on 2 December, announced that he was effectively defecting from the alliance and sought a dialogue with the Saudi-led coalition. Saleh had a long history of successfully playing Yemen's factions against each other, but in the complex environment of the war, Saleh appears to have become a proxy at least partially manipulated by external patrons. UAE Crown Prince Mohammed bin Zayed allegedly had convinced Saudi Crown Prince Mohmmad bin Salman to abandon Hadi in favor of Saleh in an effort to end the war. Through his nephew Tareq Mohammed Abdullah Saleh, head of Yemen's Special Security Forces, Saleh had established a backdoor channel with the UAE.[26] The UAE and Saleh himself seemed under the impression that Saleh's influence could muster enough forces to check Houthi power, with Tareq Saleh claiming the ability to mobilize 60,000 fighters. These developments likely emboldened Saleh in his condemnation of the Houthi, however contrary to Tareq's promises to the former president, these forces did not exist.[27] Saleh called on his loyalists to ignore Houthi orders, resulting in several days of fighting between Saleh's forces and Houthi fighters.[28] The Houthi declared Saleh and his forces "treasonous".

Ali Abdullah Saleh was killed by Houthi forces on December 4, 2017, although the exact circumstances of his death are contested. Video footage of Saleh's body showing a gunshot wound to the head was distributed on social media.[29] Some accounts report that a Houthi armored convoy assaulted Saleh and accompanying GPC leaders while they traveled from Sana'a to Saleh's hometown of Sanhan. Other accounts state that Houthi forces killed Saleh during an assault against his home in Sana'a, transporting his body into the desert to make it appear that he "had been fleeing like a coward."[30] Although pro-Saleh forces clashed with Houthi forces in the streets, leaving as many as 125 people dead according to the International Committee of the Red Cross, his murder failed to produce any large-scale revenge by loyalists. On the contrary, the Houthis were emboldened as the GPC drifted further into disarray.[31]

After the killing, thousands of Saleh loyalists including members of the family were arrested by Houthi forces. While most were released eventually, Mohammed Saleh, the late president's nephew and Tareq's brother, remained in Houthi custody as of December 2021. Tareq himself left Sana'a after his uncle's death and joined pro-Saleh forces in Hodeidah.[32] When he resurfaced the next month, Tareq released a video message calling for an end to the war while under the protection of UAE forces in the southern provinces of Mocha and Taiz.[33] He would remain as the most prominent member of the Saleh family and one which both the UAE and Saudi Arabia regarded as an ally.

The Coalition Blockade of Yemen

While Houthi forces initiated several ballistic missile attacks against targets inside Saudi Arabia as early as 2015, their longest-range missile—a Burkan-1—targeted Riyadh in May 2017, one day prior to the arrival of US President Donald Trump during his first trip overseas since assuming office (Figure 4.2).[34] In this instance, the missile was intercepted by Saudi defense forces over the Ar Rayan providence using an American-made Patriot missiles.[35] By the end of the year, the Saudi authorities claimed that Houthis had targeted Saudi territory with 83 ballistic missiles.[36] Following another thwarted missile attack targeting the Riyadh Airport in November 2017, the coalition decided to close all sea, land, and air traffic into Yemen. The near total embargo of Yemen by Saudi and coalition forces prevented much needed humanitarian aid from reaching civilians, drawing the condemnation of the United Nations resulting in some restrictions being eased.[37] Though the embargo aimed to prevent nearly all commercial imports from reaching Houthi-controlled ports, Human Rights Watch and other humanitarian organizations condemned the embargo for its "unlawfully disproportionate impact on civilians' access to essential goods", further adding that "the coalition's military strategy in Yemen has been increasingly built around preventing desperately needed aid and essential goods from reaching civilians, risking millions of lives".[38]

In its 2018 report, the United Nations Office for the Coordination of Humanitarian Affairs concluded that the blockade enforced in November 2017 further "evinced the volatility of the situation" and noted that it caused prices for consumer goods to soar, effectively putting "food, fuel and other essential items out of reach of vulnerable people overnight".[39] The UN reported 8,673 conflict-related deaths and over 58,600 injuries throughout 2017. By then, 22.2 million people including 2 million internally displaced people required humanitarian aid or protection assistance. An additional 17.8 million people were food-insecure or malnourished, including 2.9 million children and pregnant or lactating women. Half of the country's healthcare centers were no longer operational.[40] Despite its profound detrimental impact on civilians, the blockade did little to meaningfully change the military balance in the coalition's favor.

Battle of Hodeidah

In June 2018, the coalition launched an offensive to retake the port city of Hodeidah which would become one of the longest and most violent campaigns of the conflict. The fighting continued through December 2018 ending with an UN-brokered agreement in which both sides agreed to withdraw their forces from the city. From the onset, the United Nations' envoy to Yemen warned that the implications for the civilian population were high—90% of food, fuel, and medicines consumed in the country were imported with 70% coming through Hodeidah.[41] For the intervening coalition, the city was a significant source of income for Houthis and the port critical to their weapons supply. The battle for Hodeidah is visualized in Figure 4.3 to illuminate several patterns discussed next.[42]

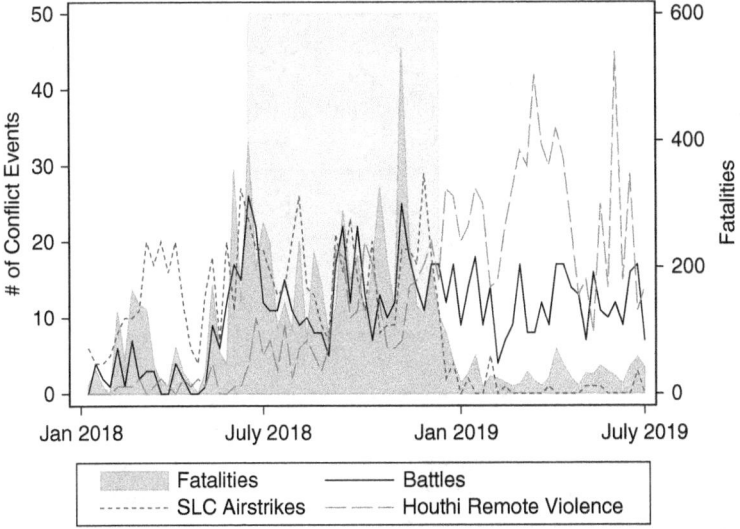

Figure 4.3 The Battle of Hodeidah, 2018.

Operation Golden Victory began on June 13, 2018. Capturing the city of 600,000 would be a formidable tactical challenge, however coalition forces and the UAE especially believed it achievable given the large advantage in combat personnel favoring the coalition: reports estimated coalition forces numbered between 21,000 and 26,500 while Houthi forces stood between 2,000 and 5,000.[43] However, the coalition advance soon stalled. The UAE's foreign minister, Anwar Gargash, tweeted that the campaign was paused in order to negotiate the terms of Houthi surrender, the reality was that Houthi defenses of the city made quick coalition conquest unlikely. While coalition forces managed to capture the airport and several small towns between Hodeidah and Mocha, to the south, Houthis fortified the city's perimeter with landmines and sniper nests making a quick advance of coalition forces difficult without incurring heavy losses.[44]

The UAE ground advance was supported by concerted Saudi airstrikes intended to soften Houthi defenses for ground units, with coalition ships positioned offshore. Houthi sources claimed that they were able to hold off coalition ships using missiles, preventing them from landing on the city's shores during the initial offensive.[45] In a speech, Abdulmalek al-Houthi urged his followers to turn the city into a "quagmire" for coalition forces.[46] Two days into the offensive, media outlets on both sides claimed tactical victories. The Houthi-controlled "Saba News Agency" quoted Houthi fighters as saying that they were "besieging the occupying forces on the western coast from a number of axies and were cutting supply routes in accordance with [their] military tactics". They claimed to have killed over 50 Yemeni government forces. UAE-based "Sky News Arabia TV" reported that Houthi suffered "heavy losses" and claimed that 128 Houthi fighters had been killed during two days of fighting.[47]

Strategically, the UAE leadership regarded tactical victories during the offensive as leverage to be applied on Houthis during peace talks. In a tweet on 17 June, UAE State Minister for Foreign Affairs Anwar Gargash declared that

> "as long as the Houthis hold [Hodeidah] they will continue to impede the political process" and that "liberating the port is the only way to bring the Houthis back to the negotiating table. The people of [Hodeidah] do not want to be governed by Iranian-backed religious extremists. They want to be free. The people of [Hodeidah] and the coalition are intent on liberating the city because it will shorten the war".[48]

While the battle for Hodeidah continued, Houthi forces continued targeting Saudi territory with ballistic missiles. When three civilians were killed in Jizan Province mid-June, the Saudi Royal Air Force stated that the missiles had deliberately targeted civilians.[49] The next day, Iranian Revolutionary Guard Corps Commander Brigadier General Mohammad Ali Jafari declared Houthi victory in the battle of Hodeidah and, in an direct threat to Saudi Arabia, reminded the Arab coalition that Iran's missiles had a range up to 2,000 km.[50] During the offensive on Hodeidah the UAE Foreign Ministry revealed that Emirati authorities had evidence of "a wide range of military weapons acquired by the Arab Coalition during operations in Yemen", showing direct Iranian support for Houthis. According to the Foreign Ministry, "the captured weapons, each of which bore distinctive links to Iran, provided physical evidence of Iranian support for the Houthi militias fighting in Yemen, and had been verified by relevant UN organizations and agencies".[51] In fact, Houthi forces had already been using these short-range missiles in their defenses of Hodeidah against both land and sea-based coalition forces.[52]

As Houthi defense held against the coalition assault and the costs imposed on the civilian population during the first weeks of fighting rapidly increased, both President Hadi and the UAE leadership were eager for a negotiated settlement. They demanded the Houthis withdraw from the city in an effort to cut off supply lines from outside backers and what the UAE Foreign Minister said was to end "profiteering from a war economy".[53] With mediation assistance from the United Nations, President Hadi and the Houthi leadership initially agreed to put the city under UN supervision.[54] However, the UN-brokered pause in hostilities did not stop coalition air strikes around Hodeidah. Just two days after the UAE announced that it was "pausing its campaign" to give the UN a chance to broker a Houthi withdrawal from the city, new air strikes targeted Houthi forces in the town of Zabid, 100-km south of the city, which led to civilian casualties.[55]

On August 9, a Saudi air-strike inside Sadaa Governorate hit a school bus killing 26 children and wounding at least 19 more. The attack was labeled a war crime by Human Rights Watch. The Saudi-led coalition insisted that strike was a "lawful attack" launched as retaliation for a ballistic missile strike inside southern Saudi Arabia the previous day. Despite evidence to the contrary, a spokesperson for Saudi Arabia denied that children were on the bus, claiming instead that the target was Houthi leaders who the coalition accused of recruiting and training young children.[56] Following months of pressure, Saudi command eventually admitted that the strike was unjustified and pledged to hold the responsible persons accountable.[57] By September, the UN mediation efforts had failed and coalition air strikes against Houthi positions inside Hodeidah had fully resumed.[58] But the coalition also set up a humanitarian corridor allowing civilians to leave the city.[59] As a result, the offensive to retake the city intensified within the city, along the Kilo 16 supply route between Hodeidah and Sana'a, and around strategic infrastructure including the airport, where Houthi forces had positioned themselves in residential areas using heavy artillery and mortar fire.[60]

Pro-government media outlets reported that government forces retook control of Kilo 16 as well as western entrances to the city by mid-September.[61] By 18 September, UAE Brigadier General Ali Al Tunaiji reported that "the Arab Coalition has launched a large-scale, multi-pronged operation toward the areas under the Houthi militias' control to liberate the city" and added that Houthi rebels' positions were "falling one by one, leading the militia forces to flee the battlefield, leaving behind their weapons, equipment and dead fighters, with Coalition forces taking control of strategic areas in Hodeidah front and cutting the rebels' supply lines".[62] Between October and November, the pro-government Giants Brigade made significant inroads into the city. As Houthi forces found themselves on the retreat inside the city, opposing media outlets reported contradictory results from the battlefield. On 10 November, the Giants Brigade Facebook page claimed they had inflicted "huge losses" upon Houthi forces and taken control of important civilian infrastructure inside the city. They also claimed that the Houthis had detonated the minaret of the Ekhwan Mosque, which Houthis had previously used as a makeshift barracks, posting images purporting to show the damage on social media.[63] The Department of Moral Guidance at the Ministry of Defense reported about "new field gains" in the city and claimed that a hospital had been liberated by the Giants Brigade although Houthi forces had detonated part of the building before their withdrawal.[64] For the most part, pro-government reporting largely centered on battlefield gains, recovery of weapons and ammunitions from enemy forces, and the number of enemy combatants killed.[65] On the other hand, the Ansar Allah Media Centre, a main Houthi-run outlet, focused on the "good tidings of victory" with daily rundowns of destroyed enemy tanks and military vehicles and on civilian victimization by pro-government and coalition forces.[66] The emphasis on purported war crimes and victimization of civilians increased as Houthi control of the city grew more tenuous. In a Washington Post op-ed, Supreme Revolutionary Committee head Mohammed Ali al-Houthi declared that his forces were ready to cease retaliatory strikes against Saudi cities while condemning Saudi aggression and US complicity of Saudi war crimes:

> The continued escalation of attacks against the port city of [Hodeidah] in Yemen by the U.S.-Saudi-Emirati coalition confirms that the American calls for a cease-fire are nothing but empty talk. The recent statements are trying to mislead the world. Saudi leaders are reckless and have no interest in diplomacy. The United States has the clout to bring an end to the conflict—but it has decided to protect a corrupt ally.[67]

On 13 December, after mediation facilitated by the United Nations in Sweden, all conflict parties committed themselves to the Stockholm Agreement which called for an immediate ceasefire in the city, a 16,000-prisoner swap, the establishment of humanitarian corridors, the agreement to withdraw all troops within 21 days, and an agreement barring them from reintroducing reinforcements to the city.[68] The Saudi coalition also agreed to a confidence-building measure, permitting an UN-chartered plane to evacuate 50 wounded Houthi fighters to Oman for medical treatment.[69] However, the truce was fragile and fighting continued across other battlefields across the country. Three weeks into the truce, each side had already accused the other of breaking it. A Houthi spokesperson claimed that their forces had respected the truce, but accused the government's forces and the coalition of 17 breaches using mortar shells and light weapons. He also added that coalition aircrafts continued fly overs. Against this stood the accusation by a coalition spokesperson accusing the Houthis of committing 138 violations since the truce came into effect.[70] In response, the UN Security Council issued Resolution 2451 on December 21, 2018, which deployed an UN monitoring team to support the immediate implementation of the ceasefire and redeployment of forces from the city and all of its ports.[71] In a subsequent resolution UNSC 2452 (2019), the Security Council established the United Nations Mission to support the Hodeidah Agreement (UNMHA) with the following mandate:

1. To lead, and support the functioning of, the Redeployment Coordination Committee (RCC), assisted by a secretariat staffed by UN personnel, to oversee the governorate-wide ceasefire, redeployment of forces, and mine action operations.
2. To monitor compliance of the parties to the ceasefire in Hodeidah governorate and the mutual redeployment of forces from the city of Hodeidah and the ports of Hodeidah, Saleef and Ras Isa.

3   To work with the parties so that security of the city of Hodeidah and the ports of Hodeidah, Saleef and Ras Isa is assured by local security forces in accordance with the Yemeni law.
4   To facilitate and coordinate UN support to assist the parties to fully implement the Hodeidah Agreement.[72]

Overall, the redeployment of forces by both parties proved difficult to implement as both feared losing control of key roads. Throughout January 2019, violent incidents between belligerents were reported in the front-line areas of the southern part of Hodeidah Governorate, along key routes running from Houthi-controlled territory in the East to territory held by pro-government forces on the western coastal strip as well as still in part of the city of Hodeidah. The Durayhimi district, located to the south of the city, remained the subject of most of the alleged incidents as both parties still controlled sections of the district along the approach to Hodeidah. Inside the city, UN observers noted significant volume of artillery fire between 13 and 14 January.[73] By February 2019, the UN had regained access to the Red Sea Mills, an important food hub and distribution facility outside Hodeidah for the first time since September 2018.[74] UN monitoring teams were only now able to inspect the facility following the demining of a section of the Sana'a-Hodeidah highway by Houthi forces. They had resisted clearing the mines to this point out of fear that it would allow enemy forces to retake the city.[75]

Houthi Drone Attacks Against Saud Arabia

Throughout spring and early summer, belligerents accused each other of exploiting the ceasefire as battles across the country continued despite it. Yemeni government officials viewed increased Houthi advances in al-Dhale and neighboring governorates as an attempt to pressure UAE backed forces in the south as to draw them away from the Red Sea theater. The Houthis, on the other hand, were perceived to be on the defensive against the Saudi-led coalitions campaigns to retake Houthi-controlled territories.[76] The most intense battles occurred between the Houthis and Hadi's Presidential Protection forces and their allied UAE-backed Security Belt force in the central Dhali province in May with several waves of offenses and counter-offensives.[77] Houthi forces also expanded their assault on Saudi infrastructure, launching multiple drone attacks including one that targeted a Saudi oil pumping station.[78] On 16 May, Saudi Arabia's Deputy Defense Minister, Khaled bin Salman, and Minister of State for Foreign Affairs, Abdel Jubeir, accused Iran publicly via tweets of having ordered the attacks. Saudi retaliatory strikes hit several military targets in Sana'a.[79] The drone attacks came a day after four ships—two Saudi tankers, one Norwegian tanker, and one Emirati tanker—were damaged in UAE coastal waters near the Strait of Hormuz.[80] Following an international investigation, the UAE, Saudi Arabia, and Norway told the United Nations Security Council that there were "strong indications that the four attacks were part of a sophisticated and coordinated operation carried out with significant operational capacity".[81] The report further found that it was "highly likely that four limpet mines, which [were] magnetically attached to a ship's hull under the waterline, were used in the attacks" and that "they had been placed by trained divers deployed from fast boats. The mines were placed soon after the ships were anchored".[82] While the report did not directly blame Iran, both the Trump administration and the Saudi government accused Iran of the attacks. Through this point in the conflict, Houthis had predominantly used artillery and missile for ranged attacks against Saudi targets. In 2019, Houthi reliance on missiles and artillery declined while their deployment of drones against Saudi Arabia increased (Figure 4.2), with attacks striking Saudi airports in Abha and Jizan in June (with one fatality) and a cruise missile strike on a power station in Jizan.[83] In July, an attack against the Abha Airport left nine civilians wounded. In August, Houthis struck the port city of Dammam with ballistic missiles, the King Khalid Airbase with a drone, as well as the Abha and Najran airports with a Houthi spokesperson confirming that the attack on Abha airport successfully "hit its targets" and disrupted air traffic.

In August, a ten-drone attack was launched against the Shaybah oil and gas field in eastern Saudi Arabia. Saudi Aramco insisted that the attack did not disrupt production or result in casualties, however a Houthi military spokesman called it the "biggest attack in the depths" of Saudi Arabia.[84] Strikes on Saudi infrastructure continued. On September 14, 2019, drone attacks caused fires at two major Aramco oil facilities, the Khrais oilfield and the Abqaiq processing facility, forcing Aramco to temporarily halt production. The Abqaiq processing facility is capable of producing 5.7 million barrels of crude per day, constituting about 5% of the global energy supply. This attack dealt a major blow to the Saudi economy, reverberating across global oil markets.[85] US Secretary of State Mike Pompeo immediately accused the Iranian government of the attack via Twitter: "Tehran is behind nearly 100 attacks on Saudi Arabia while Rouhani and Zarif pretend to engage in diplomacy. Amid all the calls for de-escalation, Iran has now launched an unprecedented attack on the world's energy supply. There is no evidence the attacks came from Yemen".[86] A United Nations inquiry (reported to the Security Council in December 2019) into the attack against Aramco concluded that one drone "traversed a location approximately 200 km (124 miles) to the northwest of the attack site" before hitting its target. Given the "900-kilometer maximum range of the Unmanned Aerial Vehicle (UAV), they concluded a high likelihood that the attack originated north of Abqaiq" making it very unlikely that the attack had originated in Yemen. The report also noted the similarities between the drones used in the Aramco attack and the Iranian-made IRN-05 UAV.[87] By June 2020, the UN Secretary General review of Iranian compliance with the 2015 Nuclear Accord assessed "that cruise missiles and/or parts thereof used in the [May and September 2019] attacks are of Iranian origin" noting that the transfer of weapons by Iran to Yemen was "inconsistent with Resolution 2231".[88] Iran denied these allegations of weapons transfers to Yemen, but also note that the 2015 resolution did not prohibit any such arms transfers.[89] The increased pace of Houthi missiles and drones attacking Saudi targets led to expanded Saudi retaliatory strikes throughout 2019 targeting in particular Sana'a and other Houthi-controlled cities.

The Coalition Split in Aden

Aden had been the base of President Hadi and allied Yemeni and coalition forces ever since Houthis took over the capital in 2015. The Hadi government was largely dysfunctional. The cabinet "governed" in exile from Saudi Arabia and the UAE leaving the bureaucracy to run itself amidst various competing factions and feuding militias. Tensions arouse between the government and southern secessionist factions after Hadi removed Aidarous al-Zoubeidi as the governor of Aden in April 2017 due to Hadi's belief that the UAE and Crown Prince Mohammed bin Zayed exerted too much influence in Yemen.[90] The dispute between Hadi and Mohammed bin Zayed largely centered around control of Aden's airport, a key supply route for Emirati-backed forces in Yemen but for the UAE more broadly. In February, the bin Zayed's own plane was denied landing at the airport and was forced to the island of Socotra instead. Notwithstanding Saudi mediation efforts, the chasm between the UAE and Hadi expanded with Hadi accusing the UAE of "behaving like an occupier of Yemen rather than its liberator" and a tweet by Dhahi Khalfan Tamim, Dubai's head of security, in which he stated that "replacing Hadi is a Gulf, Arab and international demand" adding that "the first steps toward a solution in Yemen would be to end Hadi's reign, which has eroded with time".[91] The alliance between Hadi and the UAE was effectively over.

Following al-Zoubeidi's dismissal, thousands of protesters gathered in Aden and called for him to set up "national leadership to represent the south".[92] This popular momentum coupled with support from UAE led al-Zoubeidi to form the Southern Transitional Council in May 2017. The council had representatives from each of the southern providences further isolating Hadi from southern political factions. In response, both the Gulf Cooperation Council and President Hadi immediately rejected the formation of the STC, claiming it an illegitimate effort to separate the South. Evidently, the formation of the STC also reignited decades-old call for the secession of the South.[93] The formation of the STC would transform the fight for control of Aden and cast doubt on the future of a unified Yemen. Factions previously unified in opposition to the Houthis were no longer able to manage their differences at the negotiation table and instead began fighting in the streets. By January 2018, the STC had declared a state of emergency, taken control of government offices, and openly called for an overthrow the Hadi government, accusing Hadi of having committed crimes against the people of South Yemen.[94]

Fighting between STC militias and members of Hadi's Presidential Protection Unit continued throughout the spring with the former controlling the western part of the city and the latter the eastern districts of Aden.[95] Throughout the year, ministers of the Yemeni government were unable to move freely in territory controlled by the coalition, further eroding their ability to effectively govern. Hadi himself was not permitted to return to Aden and remained in Dubai.[96] There were a series of assassinations of clerics and military and governmental officials including the security director for Aden, with no group claiming responsibility for the murders. In March 2018, the pro-southern separatist Aden al-Ghad news website reported that some 20 imams and clerics had been killed in the city and other southern provinces since 2016.[97] Other media reports put the number of assassinated clerics, preachers, and religious scholars in Aden at 25 with more than 15 having been assassinated since October 2017. Most of them were associated with the Islah Party, the Yemeni Muslim Brotherhood. The AQAP accused the UAE and their allied militias for the assassinations.[98] For their part, the STC accused the Islah Party of helping Houthis. The UAE always considered the Muslim Brotherhood, in Yemen and across the region, as a major threat to their own national security and therefore avoided contact even if it meant losing important local Hadi allies.[99]

As STC militias exerting more and more control and with the UAE restricting movement of Hadi's cabinet to and from Aden, fissures over the direction of Yemen seemed obvious to all parties involved. Saudi Arabia was more interested in balancing against Iran and denying any Houthi presence while the UAE's (in particular Abu Dhabi's) preference was the partition of Yemen as to be able to exert more control of the southern region. The extent of the patrons' influence over nearly all aspects of governance in Yemen was perhaps most apparent when Yemeni Minister of State Salah al-Sayadi was forced to resign due to pressure from Saudi Arabia and the UAE. Al Sayadi was outspoken in how he characterized the relationship between the government and coalition, which he described as "unequal and abnormal" and having transformed "from partnership to full subordination". He was instructed to leave Aden by the coalition leadership after he openly called for Yemenis to take to the streets to demand the return of President Hadi from the UAE.[100] By spring 2018, Aden's deteriorating security was entirely the product of the coalition's fissures. While the Saudis emphasized the narrative of Yemen unity from the onset of their military campaign, UAE leadership was now actively seeking southern secessionism to expand its own influence over Yemeni affairs. The UAE sought to undermine and disempower Hadi and his cabinet, and Saudi leadership seemed unable to reign in those efforts. Eager to maintain coalition cohesion, Saudis were effectively forced to witness the UAE's efforts to carve up the country. Aden and the direction of the country had fallen prey to contradictory coalition objectives.

This effectively left the country fragmented into the following competing fiefdoms:

1 The STC and other UAE-backed militias and UAE forces remained dominant in the south and effectively controlled Aden as they remained the most powerful military force.
2 The Yemeni government's seat remained in Aden, but Hadi and his cabinet were largely confined to exile in the UAE.
3 Houthis remained in control of the north-west, including Sana'a.
4 Factions associated with the Hadi government aligned with Saudi Arabia were dominant in Marib, east of Sana'a.[101]

The truce in Aden, brokered by Saudi Arabia and UAE, was fragile and in the absence of both political reconciliation of local factions and unified coalition objectives, the city, and by extension the entire government remained dysfunctional. On a visit to Aden in 2018, the International Crisis Group's director for the Persian Gulf described the situation as follows:

The city is held hostage by an interconnected tug of war between, on the one hand, Hadi government supporters and their STC opponents and, on the other, between competing national and local government interests, with all seeking control over resources and none effectively governing. ... No foreign diplomatic missions are operating. The Adenis are starting to resent the inattention, from the UAE in particular, which residents say is overly focused on narrow security concerns, and especially counter-terrorism. The Emiratis were once viewed as liberators, but now the term "occupation" is in the air. I heard a lot of this talk even from people who are not on the side of the Hadi government.[102]

The battle over control of Aden, and by extension over the South, culminated in August 2019 after the death of Southern Security Belt commander Brigadier General Munir Mahmoud Ahmad al-Mashali (more commonly known as al-Yafei) by a Houthi-claimed missile strike during a military graduation ceremony on 1 August. Nine days later STC militias took full control over Aden's military bases and government institutions.[103] When government-aligned forces moved to Aden in an attempt to retake the city, the UAE designated them as "terrorist militias" launching air strikes in "self-defense".[104] Prior to these clashes, the Emirates actually cut their deployments around Hodeidah by 80% to fewer than 150 troops. They also had pulled out attack helicopters, Patriot Systems, and other heavy guns from Yemen. While a UAE official said the "strategic redeployment" was intended to support the UN-brokered ceasefire in Hodeidah, the decision seemed to reflect the Emirate leadership's realization that the military campaign was more of quagmire than a winnable war.[105] While officials in both the UAE and Saudi Arabia publicly downplayed the drawdown's impact on coalition strategy, Saudi diplomats privately expressed their disappointment. According to a Western diplomat, senior Saudi officials within the royal court personally intervened with the Emirati leaders to try to dissuade them from the withdrawal.[106]

Pro-governmental forces sought to regain control of Aden throughout 2019. While the UAE and Saudi Arabia publicly called for a dialogue to end the infighting, the Yemeni government criticized UAE as "fully responsible for the armed rebellion".[107] By October, Riyadh had deployed forces to replace UAE troops at the city's airport and military bases, followed by an official handover of security responsibilities in the city and its suburbs to Saudi command.[108] On November 5, 2019, an agreement was reached for power sharing that included the STC as part of the government and called for the demilitarization of Aden and the integration of militias and paramilitary groups under the auspices of the defense and interior ministries.[109] Yet the agreement was never implemented, but rather failed to what one observer called the "vagueness and the conflicting agendas of the UAE and the Saudis at the time".[110] STC military forces were disarmed and be integrated with governmental forces prior to the formation of the unified political apparatus, creating vulnerabilities for the STC were the government to renege. This did not happen within the agreed-to timeframe.[111] In fact, the STC continuously and openly violated those stipulations, often engaging in hostile rhetoric toward the government and even declaring "autonomous rule in the South" in April 2020.[112] In June, southern separatist militias seized control of Socotra, an island in the Gulf of Aden. Socotra's governor, Ramzi Mahroos, accused both the Saudi and the UAE governments of turning a blind eye to what the Hadi government called a "fully fledged coup".[113] It was not until December 2020 that Hadi announced the formation of a new cabinet which would include the STC without forcing them have previously met military and security obligations. The incorporation of the STC into the government provided for a truce between the factions and it gave the STC de facto political recognition and a seat the UN-sponsored negotiation table over the future of the country.[114] Although the STC did not implement the agreed-to security provisions (with the exception of bilateral redeployments of forces in the frontlines of across Abyan Province), the Hadi government considered the agreement with the STC a victory over the UAE, whose influence and presence in the south had been significantly reduced. To Hadi, incorporating the STC into the government was an act of coopting the STC and ultimately checking their separatist ambitions.[115]

Continuation of Border War with Saudi Arabia

By 2020, Yemen was effectively split into the four areas of political and military control. Fighting between factions cut off roads and divided control of the country's seaports and airports. On 3 January, US President Donald Trump ordered the assassination of Islamic Revolutionary Guard Corps-General Qasem Soleimani via drone strike in Iraq. While the White House initially justified the killing to prevent "an imminent attack against US personnel and embassies", Secretary of State Pompeo would eventually called it part of a larger strategy of "deterrence".[116] On the same day, US forces also attempted but failed to assassinate Abdul Reza Shahlai, who US authorities designated as financier and key commander in Iran's Quds Force in Yemen.[117] Soleimani's death and that of an Iraqi militia leader prompted demonstrations against the United States in Sana'a and Saada region and promises of revenge from the Houthi leadership.[118]

Following US raids, the Saudi-led coalition stepped up air strikes against Houthi forces in the North, ultimately prompting renewed cross-border attacks. In Marib, 116 Yemeni troops were killed when Houthi-launched ballistic missiles hit a mosque at al-Estiqbal military camp during evening prayers. Fierce fighting between government forces and Houthis resumed shortly thereafter, centered around a junction east of Marib that connected the province to Sana'a. Saudi air strikes hit Sana'a and Saada provinces, both held by Houthis.[119] On 14 February, Houthis claimed responsibility for downing a Saudi military jet in Al-Jawf governorate prompting retaliatory air strikes in Al-Jawf the next day that killed 31 civilians, 26 of which were children.[120] Despite discission between the Yemeni government, the Saudis, and Houthis on confidence-building measures in Amman, cross-border attacks between Houthis and Saudis significantly increased during this period.[121]

The Al-Jawf Offensive and the 2020 Pandemic

On 1 March 2020, Houthis took the strategic northern city Hazm, the capital of Al-Jawf province and a key supply line linking Marib with Jawf, located along the border with Saudi Arabia. The takeover of Hazm put Houthis closer to the central province of Marib, which was at the time the only safe area in the country for those opposing the Houthis.[122] The Houthi take-over of Hazm following weeks of siege was facilitated by the support of local tribal leaders. As a Houthi member told an outlet: "Al-Jawf is one of the most important provinces for us as there are some loyal tribal leaders there who asked us to liberate the province and our forces were brave enough to do so".[123] Pro-government forces in Hazm had abandoned their fighting positions leaving only tribal militias to defend the city. Houthis allowed for the safe passage for the governor to leave the city. Pro-Hadi officials considered the fall of Hazm to be a betrayal by the Saudi-led coalition and officials outside of the country who had the capabilities to reinforce Hazm, although locals blamed the weakened government and army, accusing both of "playing with the souls of the tribes".[124] The military balance now clearly favored Houthis. By and large, Houthi forces had emerged as the superior fighting force throughout the country, putting government forces and their outside patrons on the defensive.

The Houthi campaign to take over Yemen would face little meaningful resistance until the global coronavirus pandemic reached Yemen. Following the first case of COVID in Saudi Arabia and a global appeal by the Secretary General of the United Nations to all belligerents to lay down their weapons in order to help halt the spread of the virus, the Saudi government announced a two-week-long unilateral ceasefire on April 9, 2020.[125] The UN's Special Envoy to Yemen hoped the ceasefire might be an opportunity for progress in peace-talks. Instead, it would only exacerbate the already dire humanitarian situation in the country by imposing an additional layer of hardship onto the Yemeni people. Just like humanitarian aid, the distribution of COVID vaccines was weaponized by belligerents.[126] By May 2021, Yemen had access to vaccine doses to cover about to 20% of its population through the COVAX initiative. The government had pledged to distribute the vaccine in the country's most populated areas, but those areas were all controlled by Houthis.[127] By spring of 2022, Yemeni health authorities had administered over 807,000 doses of COVID vaccines, amounting to only 1.4% of the population. Meanwhile, there had been over 11,800 reported cases of COVID resulting in at least 2,143 deaths.[128] For the majority of the country's population, safe access to government-controlled hospitals where vaccines were available for those living in Houthi-controlled areas remained largely elusive.[129]

As noted above, the pandemic saw no meaningful breakthroughs in peace negotiations or diplomatic efforts, which remained largely stalled throughout 2020. By late fall, the humanitarian situation had declined so significantly that the UN Secretary-General warned that the country was "in imminent danger of the worst famine the world has seen for decades".[130] In the northern parts of Yemen, the belligerent forces had remained locked in a stalemate with neither side making progress along the most active battlefronts in Marib and Al-Jawf Governorates. Then, Houthi offensive seized the Mas military camp west of Marib giving them strategic control of the high ground overseeing the main highway leading to the last major urban stronghold held by government forces.[131] During the offensive, Houthis claimed to have killed several Saudi soldiers stationed in the Marib governorate.[132] In October, a prisoner exchange involving over 1,000 prisoners occurred. It was praised by the UN Security Council as an "airlift of hope". Houthi forces continued cross-border attacks into Saudi Arabia, including the targeting another Aramco oil facility on 23 November, immediately following US Secretary of State Mike Pompeo's visit to the kingdom.[133]

Aden Airport Attack 2020

By the end of December 2020, the 2019 Saudi-brokered power-sharing agreement between Hadi and the STC finally went into effect. Hadi and the new 24-member cabinet were in Riyadh for a swearing in ceremony. Hadi would continue to serve as president, and Prime Minister Maeen Abdul Malik would lead the new cabinet comprised of equal members from the northern and southern regions.[134] As the new government returned to Aden, three missiles hit the airport, killing 20 people including the Deputy Minister of Public Works and injuring more than 100 others. Both the UN Secretary General the special envoy to Yemen immediately condemned "the deplorable attack", wished the Cabinet "strength in facing the difficult tasks ahead", and called it an "unacceptable act of violence [that] is a tragic reminder of the importance of bringing Yemen urgently back on the path toward peace".[135] A report submitted to the UN Security Council in March 2021 concluded that "the airport was hit by three precision-guided, short-distance, surface-to-surface ballistic missiles carrying fragmentation warheads, likely an extended-range version of the Badr-1P missile, which has been part of the Houthi arsenal since 2018".[136] In addition to the plane carrying the new cabinet members, the report concluded that the airport's VIP lounge, where a press conference had been planned, had also been targeted. The origins of the attack were "facilities were under the control of the Houthi forces at the time of the attacks".[137] The attack demonstrated Houthis' advanced tactical and intelligence capabilities, as well as their willingness to pursue maximalist goals on the battlefield.

US Designation of Houthis as Terrorists

Throughout US President Trump's tenure, his administration's "maximum pressure" campaign against Iran translated into the containment of Iranian support for Houthis as well as increased military and political support for Saudi Arabia. Notwithstanding accusations of Saudi war crimes as well as the assassination of Washington Post journalist Jamal Khashoggi in the Saudi consulate in Istanbul in 2018, President Trump held on to support Riyadh's war efforts in Yemen. Like his predecessor, the Trump administration continued to act as super-patron toward the Saudi coalition. Yet as is often the case in a proxy war setting, the United States' strategic objectives were external to the underlying war. Rather than pushing the belligerents toward a peaceful resolution, they instead worked through Saudi and UAE military power to balance against Iran. This context frames US Secretary of States Pompeo's final official act; just one day before President Joseph Biden was inaugurated, the US government designated the Houthis as a "foreign terrorist organization" in an attempt to force the incoming Biden administration to maintain the status quo. The designation was almost universally decried by humanitarian organizations. The United Nations envoy in Yemen, UN Humanitarian Affairs chief and Emergency Coordinator, and head of the World Food Program all urged the US government to reverse the decision due to the anticipated impact on humanitarian assistance.[138] Only three weeks later on 12 February, the Biden administration revoked the terrorist organization designation citing those concerns.

The new US Secretary of State Anthony Blinken explained that "the revocations are intended to ensure that relevant US policies do not impede assistance to those already suffering what has been called the world's worst humanitarian crisis. By focusing on alleviating the humanitarian situation in Yemen, we hope the Yemeni parties can also focus on engaging in dialogue".[139] Additionally, the United States would continue to "monitor the activities" of Houthi leadership and were identifying additional targets for designation, "especially those responsible for explosive boat attacks against commercial shipping in the Red Sea and UAV and missile attacks into Saudi Arabia".[140] President Biden simultaneously announced an end to the US government's support for Saudi Arabia's war efforts. Speaking to the Department of State, Biden said that "this war has to end" ... "and to underscore our commitment, we're ending all American support for offensive operations in the war in Yemen, including relevant arms sales".[141] Two pending sales of precision-guided munitions were halted. Yet the administration's policy reversal was also largely rhetorical intended for domestic audiences within the United States. Although offensive support would stop, the United States remained committed to Saudi defense. Moreover, most "defensive" weapons platforms have offensive applications, providing an easy workaround. Biden reiterated the importance of "defending" Saudi Arabia as a means to contain Iran, adding that "Saudi Arabia faces missile attacks, UAV (drone) strikes and other threats from Iranian-supplied forces in multiple countries. We're going to continue to support and help Saudi Arabia defend its sovereignty and its territorial integrity and its people".[142]

On 10 February, Houthis targeted an airport in southwestern Saudi Arabia with a bomb-laden drone, punching a hole through the fuselage of an Airbus A-320.[143] By the end of the year, the Department of State would approve Saudi Arabia's first major weapons deal under the Biden administration: 280 air-to-air missiles valued at up to $650 million. The proposed deal received bipartisan confidence when the Senate voted down an effort to block the sale over Saudi Arabia's human rights record and alleged war crimes in the conflict with a 67-to-30 supermajority.[144]

Houthi Gains and Elusiveness of Peace

Throughout 2021, Houthis consolidated their hold on territories in central Yemen while expanding their offensives into government-controlled territory and key energy-producing regions. They also escalated cross-border attacks into Saudi territory.[145] Following the reduction of US support, Saudi leadership was keen on ending the conflict while maintaining a veneer of victory. A Saudi peace proposal was forwarded to Houthis on March 22, 2021 that centered around previous UN initiatives but also expanded the US government's role in helped implement the proposal.[146] The Saudi roadmap included a UN-supervised ceasefire, measures to reopen Sana'a airport in the Yemeni capital, and the lifting of trade restrictions on the government-controlled Hodeidah port followed by talks between the Houthis and the government for a more enduring political solution.[147] Houthis rejected the proposal on grounds of timing, sequencing, and the particulars of proposed terms. As Peter Salisbury from the Crisis Group noted on Twitter:

> But whereas the Houthis want Hodeidah port and Sana'a airport to be completely open to all international traffic, the Saudi proposal envisages a role for the Yemeni government in regulating both—and for a ceasefire to come before any economic or humanitarian assistance. The proposal also suggests the sharing of revenues on trade in oil through Hodeidah.[148]

From the Houthis' perspective, all of the concessions would come from them.[149] Accordingly, Houthi official Mohammed al-Bukaiti rejected the cease-fire offer, citing the Saudi-led coalition's continued closure of the airport in Sana'a and restrictions on the country's ports. Accusing Saudis of using the humanitarian situation as leverage, Al-Bkaiti posted on Twitter: "If the blockade is not lifted, the declaration of the coalition of aggression to stop its military operations will be meaningless because the suffering of Yemenis as a result of the blockade is more severe than the war itself".[150]

The country's military balance largely stood in the Houthi's favor and their leadership clearly saw any agreement that would require giving up territory as unacceptable. For most of 2021, Houthis continued with offensives pushing into government-controlled territory. By October

2021, Houthis had consolidated their hold upon al-Bayda, a strategically located governorate in central Yemen, and continued their strategy of "pushing into government-controlled territory to isolate, eliminate or co-opt tribal and other rivals".[151] By the end of the year, the city of Marib remained surrounded by Houthi forces.

Conclusion

By all accounts, the Saudi-led intervention into the war failed to produce Riyadh's desired outcome. Seven years of war neither reinstated the Yemeni government nor did it succeed in balancing against Iran by means of fighting Houthi forces. On the contrary, the military balance tilted to the favor of Houthis. Furthermore, the expanding divisions within the coalition undermined coalition effectiveness and offset any progress on the battlefield or in the regional political theater. These fissures impacted the conflict's trajectory enough to create an apparent decoupling of the Saudi-led coalition's targeting and applications of force from the actual progression of the on-the-ground war. Figure 4.4 presents the war in Yemen from three vantage points: severity, intensity, and external intrusions. Each of the stacked bands shows the monthly fatality levels, numbers of battle-days, and number of coalition air strikes reported by ACLED in each Yemeni Governorate over the seven-year span of the war.[152] Throughout the entirety of the war, fatalities within governorates tracks closely with battle frequency. For the initial three years of conflict, coalition air strikes also appear to track battlefield progress, with the notable exception of coalition air strikes targeting Saada along the border with Saudi Arabia. However, as the intensity and lethality of fighting increases expeditiously in 2018, coalition air strikes—especially those where pro-regime forces are actively engaging Houthi forces in battle—decrease and all but disappear with Saada again being the lone exception. As discussed earlier and at length in the next chapter, this decrease corresponds with the emerging schism between UAE and Saudi Arabia as southern Yemeni governorates seek greater autonomy in addition to increased scrutiny of the Saudi-American partnership following the assassination of American-based journalist Jamal Khashoggi that limited the transfer of American weaponry to the Kingdom in 2019.

In the broader regional setting, these fissures within the coalition strengthened Houthis and by extension Iranian influence in Yemen. Despite billions of dollars of US military equipment sold to Saudi Arabia over decades, the Saudi military was unable to translate its firepower advantage into any meaningful coercive strategy. They failed

Key Military Engagements in Yemen 63

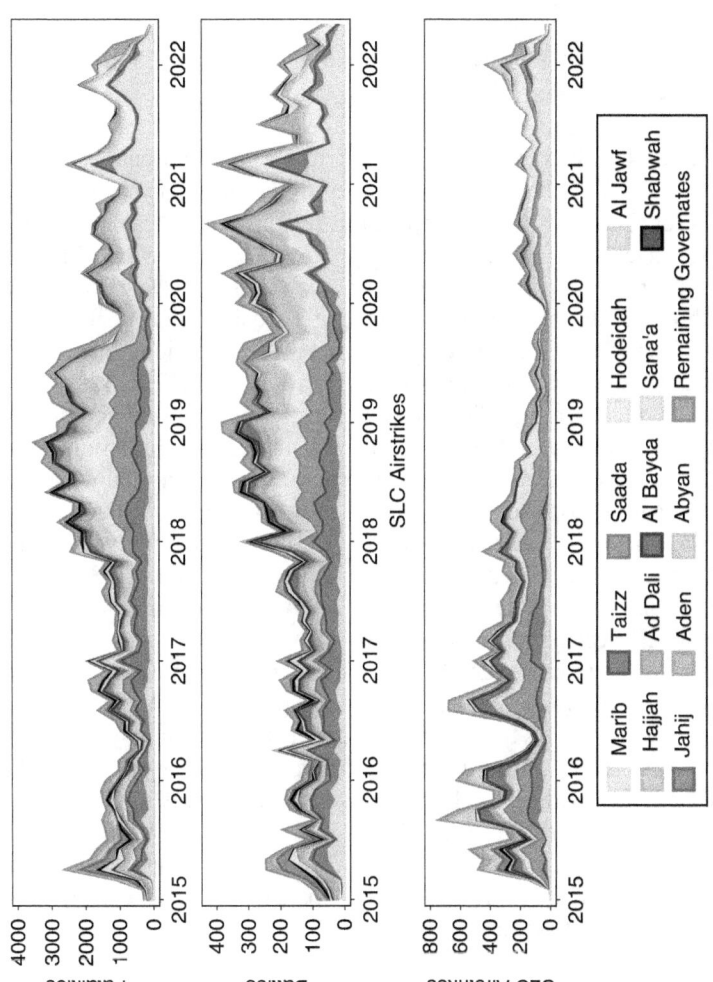

Figure 4.4 Battles, Air Strikes, and Fatalities in Yemen, 2015–2022.

to defeat Houthi forces and they failed to weaken Iran. The Iranian government, on the other hand, successfully bled Saudi resources during years of conflict, and while they entered the war on the side of the Houthis, they did so almost entirely covertly allowing them to cast Saudi Arabia as the aggressor and themselves as merely providing aid to a country under attack.

The war in Yemen has been fought during a time of extensive violent upheavals and conflicts throughout the Middle East. The fallout of the Arab Spring has not only caused over a decade of revolutions, political violence and civil war, but it also led to the internationalization of intrastate conflict. The conflicts in Iraq, Syria, and Libya all became international conflict theaters with both regional and great powers intervening against an ever-growing transnational jihadi network. Moving between conflicts, fighters and professional mercenaries were exposed to a plethora of asymmetrical warfare tactics, combat experience, and criminal networks. This loose confederacy of transnational jihadi networks contributed to total warfare in Syria and give rise to ISIS while also exporting terrorist cells to Europe. More than just expanding terrorist and criminal networks, more than a decade of asymmetrical warfare in Iraq and Afghanistan has demonstrated yet again that insurgents can outlast occupying forces—to win a civil war, all the rebels must do is not lose. The US withdrawal from Iraq and in particular the exit from Afghanistan demonstrated to US enemies that the US military will eventually capitulate and leave. It demonstrates that US efforts at political engineering through military power cannot be maintained amidst ongoing violence. Leaders in Iran interpreted these developments as signs of decreasing US power projection capabilities within the region and were able to use Iran's strength and experience in asymmetrical warfare as leverage during negotiations over its nuclear program. The IRGC together with Shi'a Iraqis proved fundamental to the United States in defeating ISIS in Iraq. By the same token, the IRGC directly worked against US interests in the Yemeni theater. While the Taliban outlasted US and NATO forces in Afghanistan, the Houthis (supported by Iran) seem on track to outendure the Saudis in Yemen.

Notes

1 BBC Monitoring, "Iran Official Slams Saudi "Illogical, Imperialist Policies", *E'temad,* BBC Monitoring (21 May 2015).
2 BBC Monitoring, Deputy Chief of Staff of the Iranian Armed Forces Brigadier General Massud Jazayeri called on the US and its allies to "avoid double-standard measures in Yemen and (recognize and) respect the Yemeni people's legitimate demands", BBC Monitoring.

3 BBC Monitoring 2015.
4 BBC Monitoring, "Top Iranian Cleric Asks Foreign Ministry to Use "Strong Diplomacy" in Yemen", *Islamic Republic News Agency*, BBC Monitoring (16 April 2015).
5 See statements by Chief of Staff of the Iranian Armed Forces, Major General Hasan Firuzabadi, BBC Monitoring Saudi Claims of Iran Flows to Yemen "ridiculous" – commander, *ISNA*, BBC Monitoring (18 April 2015).
6 See statement by Iran's Deputy Foreign Minister for Arab and African Affairs Hossein Amir-Abdollahian, BBC Monitoring Saudi War on Yemen Endangers regional security: Iran Deputy Foreign Minister, IRNA, BBC Monitoring (14 April 2015).
7 Kareem Shaheen, "Yemen: Houthi Fighters 'Seize Presidential Palace' in Battle for Aden", *The Guardian* (2 April 2015), https://www.theguardian.com/world/2015/apr/02/yemen-houthi-fighters-aden-southern-port-crater-saudi (accessed 29 September 2021).
8 See statement by Adel bin Ahmed Al-Jubeir, Saudi ambassador to the US, BBC Monitoring, Saudi Ambassador to USA battle of Yemen between good and evil, Jedda (4 April 2015) BBC Monitoring.
9 Ibid.
10 Clionadh Raleigh, Andrew Linke, Håvard Hegre and Joakim Karlsen (2010). "Introducing ACLED: An Armed Conflict Location and Event Dataset: Special Data Feature". *Journal of Peace Research* 47 (5): 651–60, https://doi.org/10.1177/0022343310378914. All analyses reliant on ACLED's data use the May 20, 2022 version of the Middle East Regional data file.
11 Battles include all recorded battles regardless of participants, while air strikes only include those assigned directly to Operation Decisive Storm or initiated by members of the Saudi-led coalition.
12 Fatih Bin-Lazrq and Kareem Fahim, "Yemen's Despair on Full Display in Ruined City", *The New York Times* (10 April 2015), https://www.nytimes.com/2015/04/11/world/middleeast/aden-yemen.html (accessed 12 October 2021).
13 SIPRI, Stockholm International Peace Research Institute, Yemen (NGF), https://www.sipri.org/databases/embargoes/un_arms_embargoes/yemen/yemen (13 June 2019) (accessed 1 November 2021).
14 ACLED, "The Wartime Transformation of AQAP in Yemen" (14 December 2020), https://www.jstor.org/stable/resrep28722 (accessed 12 November 2021); al-Qaeda defends Yemen's al-Mukalla as tribesmen fail to enter city, Yemen Times (6 April 2015) BBC Monitoring.
15 Reuters, "Houthi Shells Kill 5 in Saudi Border Town", *Reuters* (6 May 2015), https://www.reuters.com/article/us-yemen-security-saudi-border/houthi-shells-kill-five-in-saudi-border-town-idUSKBN0NR20S20150506 (accessed 12 November 2021).
16 We include all "remote violence" events attributed to Houthi actors occurring within Saudi territory, subdivided by the type of attack. We also include as a separate category "disrupted weapons use" within Saudi Arabia which include failed attacks intercepted by Saudi defense forces.
17 ACLED, The Saudi – Yemeni Border Conflict, https://acleddata.com/2018/07/13/the-saudi-yemeni-border-conflict/ (accessed 12 November 2021).

18 By September 2015, 45 Emirate soldiers died in a missile strike by Houthi forces, as well as 10 Saudi and 5 Bahraini soldiers also died in the attack. BBC, "Yemen Crisis: UAE Launches Fresh Yemen Attacks" (5 September 2015), https://www.bbc.com/news/world-middle-east-34163982 (accessed 12 November 2021); AFP Riyadh, "Saudi General Killed near Yemen Border" (27 September 2015), https://english.alarabiya.net/News/middle-east/2015/09/27/Saudi-general-killed-near-Yemen-border- (accessed 21 November 2021).
19 Hugh Naylor, "Saudi-Led Coalition Plans Ground Attacks in Yemen after Taking Key City", *The Washington Post* (29 July 2015), https://www.washingtonpost.com/world/middle_east/saudi-led-coalition-plans-ground-attacks-in-yemen-after-taking-key-city/2015/07/28/a2131646-315d-11e5-a879-213078d03dd3_story.html (accessed 19 November 2021).
20 Ali al-Mujahed and Hugh Taylor, "Embattled President Hadi Returns to Yemen after Six-Month Exile", *The Washington Post* (22 September 2015), https://www.washingtonpost.com/world/middle_east/embattled-president-hadi-returns-to-yemen-after-six-month-exile/2015/09/22/6f2861e5-a9b8-4eb5-9cac-81864f4ab42a_story.html (accessed 12 November 2021).
21 Interview with author.
22 BBC Monitoring, "Saudi FM Rejects "One-Side" Yemeni Houthi-Dominated Council", *al-Arabiya* (25 August 2016).
23 Al-Jazeera, "Yemen's Saleh Stages Mass Rally amid Houthi Rift", *al-Jazeera* (24 August 2017), https://www.aljazeera.com/news/2017/8/24/yemens-saleh-stages-mass-rally-amid-houthi-rift (accessed 4 December 2021).
24 Ibid.
25 Reuters, "Houthi and Saleh Forces Clash in Sanaa, at least 2 Dead", *Reuters* (26 August 2017), https://www.reuters.com/article/yemen-security-idINKCN1B7026 (accessed 1 December 2021); interview with author.
26 Interview with author.
27 Interview with author.
28 Faisal Edroos, "How Did Yemen's Houthi-Saleh Alliance Collapse?", *al-Jazeera* (4 December 2017), https://www.aljazeera.com/news/2017/12/4/how-did-yemens-houthi-saleh-alliance-collapse (accessed 12 November 2021).
29 Sami Aboudi and Noah Brownig, "Exiled Son of Yemen's Saleh Takes up Anti-Houthi Cause", *Reuters* (4 December 2017), https://www.reuters.com/article/us-yemen-security/saudi-warplanes-strike-houthis-as-alliances-shift-in-yemen-war-idUSKBN1DY12V; Patrick Wintour, "Yemebn Houthis Kill Former President Ali Abullah Saleh", *The Guardian* (4 December 2017), https://www.theguardian.com/world/2017/dec/04/former-yemen-president-saleh-killed-in-fresh-fighting (accessed 20 November 2021). It remains unclear whether Saleh was killed on route or at his compound in Aden.
30 Shuaib Almosawa and Ben Hubbard, "Yemen's Ex-President Killed as Mayhem Convulses Capital", *The New York Times* (4 December 2017), https://www.nytimes.com/2017/12/04/world/middleeast/saleh-yemen-houthis.html (accessed 1 December 2021).
31 Ibid.
32 Interview with author.

Key Military Engagements in Yemen 67

33 Middle East Eye, "A Killer or a Hero? Nephew of Former Yemeni President Divides Taiz" (31 May 2018), https://www.middleeasteye.net/news/killer-or-hero-nephew-former-yemeni-president-divides-taiz (accessed 3 December 2021).
34 Al-Jazeera, "Yemen Rebel Missile Shot Down 200 km from Saudi Capital", *al-Jazeera* (20 May 2017), https://www.aljazeera.com/news/2017/5/20/yemen-rebel-missile-shot-down-200km-from-saudi-capital (accessed 18 December 2021).
35 Ibid; the Houthis acknowledged firing the missile and stated that the target had been a palace of King Salman. Ben Hubbard and Nick Cumming-Bruce, "Rebels in Yemen Fire Second Ballistic Missile at Saudi Capital", *The New York Times* (19 December 2017), https://www.nytimes.com/2017/12/19/world/middleeast/yemen-rebels-missile-riyadh.html (accessed 29 December 2021).
36 BBC Monitoring, "Houthis Fired 83 Ballistic Missiles at Saudi, Coalition Says", *BBC Monitoring* (20 December 2017).
37 Human Rights Watch, "Yemen: Coalition Blockade Imperils Civilians", (7 December 2017), https://www.hrw.org/news/2017/12/07/yemen-coalition-blockade-imperils-civilians (accessed 29 December 2021).
38 Ibid.
39 United Nations Office for the Coordination of Humanitarian Affairs, "Global Humanitarian Overview: 2018", https://reliefweb.int/sites/reliefweb.int/files/resources/GHO2018.PDF (accessed 29 December 2021).
40 Ibid.
41 Euan McKirdy, "Saudi-Led Forces Began Attack on Yemen Port City, Ignoring UN Warnings", *CNN* (13 June 2018) https://www.cnn.com/2018/06/13/middleeast/yemen-hodeidah-attack-intl/index.html
42 We graph weekly aggregates of fatalities and conflict events occurring in the Hodeidah Governorate between January 2018 through July 2019 as reported by the ACLED project. The shaded area indicates the period between the June 13th commencement of the SLC's offensive and the December 13th brokered ceasefire.
43 ACLED, "The Battle of Houdeidah Has Started" (22 June 2018), https://acleddata.com/2018/06/21/the-battle-of-hodeidah-has-started/ (accessed 12 January 2022).
44 Middle East Eye, "Stalemate in Yemen: Why Has the Battle for Hodeidah Ground to a Halt?" (27 July 2018), https://www.middleeasteye.net/news/stalemate-yemen-why-has-battle-hodeidah-ground-halt (accessed 12 January 2022).
45 Dion Nissenbaum and Margherita Stancati, "Yemeni Forces, Backed by Saudi-Led Coalition, Launch Assault on Country's Main Port", *The Wallstreet Journal* (13 June 2018), https://archive.ph/20180613182724/https://www.wsj.com/articles/yemeni-forces-backed-by-saudi-led-coalition-launch-assault-on-countrys-main-port-1528870659#selection-2103.0–2103.83 (accessed 18 January 2021).
46 BBC Monitoring, "Rebel Leader Vows to Turn Yemeni Port into 'Quagmire' for Saudi-Led Forces" (15 June 2018).
47 BBC Monitoring, "Yemen's Houthis Kill 50 Rival Forces in Hudaydah Battles" (16 June 2018).

48 BBC Monitoring, "UAE Stresses Importance of Control over Hudaydah" (17 June 2018); al-Jazeera, "Saudi Arabia: Houthi Missiles Attack Kills Three in Jizan" (10 June 2018), https://www.aljazeera.com/news/2018/6/10/saudi-arabia-houthi-missile-attack-kills-three-in-jizan (accessed 18 January 2022).

49 BBC Monitoring, "Yemen Houthi Missile Fired into Saudi Arabia Injures One", SPA News Agency (18 June 2018).

50 BBC Monitoring, "Yemen's Houthis Close to Victory, Iran Guard Chief Says", *ISNA* (19 June 2018).

51 BBC Monitoring, "UAE Acquires 'Evidence' of Iranian Support for Houthi Militia", *al-Bayan* (20 June 2018).

52 For example, on 30 June, Houthi-controlled Saba News Agency reported that the rebels "had fired a short-range missile on "gatherings of invaders and mercenaries" and shelled positions of the pro-government forces backed by the Saudi-led coalition, killing and injuring some and destroying their equipment". BBC Monitoring, "Yemen's Houthis Launch Ballistic amid Ongoing Hudaydah Battle" (30 June 2018).

53 BBC Monitoring, "UAE Says Hudaydah 'Liberation' Essential for UN-Led Effort" (27 June 2018).

54 BBC Monitoring, "Yemen's Houthi Rebels Agree to UN Control of Hudaydah" (17 June 2018).

55 BBC Monitoring, "Air Strikes near Yemen's Houdeydah after UAE 'Pause'" (3 July 2018).

56 Human Rights Watch, "Yemen: Coalition Bus Bombing Apparent War Crime" (2 September 2018), https://www.hrw.org/news/2018/09/02/yemen-coalition-bus-bombing-apparent-war-crime# (accessed 24 January 2022).

57 Reuter, "Saudi-Led Coalition Admits Deadly Yemen Strike on Bus Was Unjustified" (1 September 2018), https://www.reuters.com/article/us-yemen-security-saudi-strike/deadly-yemen-air-strike-on-bus-was-unjustified-coalition-team-idUSKCN1LH3JO?il=0 (accessed 24 January 2018).

58 BBC Monitoring, "Coalition Jet Bomb Houthi Positions in Key Yemen Port City" (22 September 2018).

59 BBC Monitoring, Saudi news outlet, al-Arabiya claimed a majority of the tens of thousands of civilians who fled the city and its surroundings were living in camps set up by the King Salman Centre and the UAE Red-Crescent. "Saudi-Led Coalition to Set Up Hudaydah Humanitarian Exits" (23 September 2018).

60 BBC Monitoring, "Fighting Resumes Between Army, Houthi Forces in Hudaydah", *al-Masdar* (29 September 2018).

61 BBC Monitoring, "Yemen Army Cuts Off Houthi Suppl Line as Hudaydah Battle Rages" (12 September 2018).

62 BBC Monitoring, "UAE Says Arab Coalition Launches Operation in Yemen's Hudaydah", WAM News Agency (18 September 2018).

63 BBC Monitoring, "Contradictory Reports as Battle for Yemen's Hudaydah Rages" (10 November 2018).

64 Ibid.

65 BBC Monitoring, "Fresh Clashes as Yemen Warring Sides Fight in Hudaydah" (3 November 2018).

66 BBC Monitoring, "Contradictory Reports as Battle for Yemen's Hudaydah Rages".

67 Mohammed Ali al-Houthi, "We Want Peace for Yemen, But Saudi Airstrikes Must Stop", *The Washington Post* (9 November 2018), https://www.washingtonpost.com/news/global-opinions/wp/2018/11/09/houthi-leader-we-want-peace-for-yemen-but-saudi-airstrikes-must-stop/ (accessed 12 January 2022).
68 Patrick Wintour and Bethan McKernan, "Yemen: Ceasefire Agreed for Port City", *The Guardian* (13 December 2018), https://www.theguardian.com/world/2018/dec/13/yemen-ceasefire-agreed-for-vital-port-city-of-hodeidah (accessed 29 January 2022).
69 France 24, "Wounded Houthi Fighters to Be Evacuated from Yemen, Says Saudi Coalition" (12 December 2018), https://www.france24.com/en/20181203-wounded-houthi-fighters-be-evacuated-yemen-says-saudi-coalition-peace-talks (accessed 29 January 2022).
70 BBC Monitoring, "Yemen Rivals Continue to Clash as UN Envoy Visits Hudaydah" (25 December 2018); UN Security Council, Letter dated 20 December 2018 from the Secretary-General addressed to the President of the Council (20 December 2018) S/2018/1134, https://undocs.org/en/S/2018/1134 (accessed 29 January 2022).
71 UN Security Council Resolution 2451 (2018) S/RES/2451 (2018), https://undocs.org/S/RES/2451(2018) (accessed 29 January 2022).
72 UN Department of Political and Peacebuilding Affairs, UNMHA, Hudaydah Agreement (16 January 2019), https://dppa.un.org/en/mission/unmha-hudaydah-agreement (accessed 29 January 2022).
73 UN Security Council, "Status of Implementation of Security Council Resolution 2451 – Report by the Secretary General S/2019/69" (21 January 2019), https://www.securitycouncilreport.org/atf/cf/%7B65BFCF9B-6D27-4E9C-8CD3-CF6E4FF96FF9%7D/s_2019_69.pdf (accessed 29 January 2022).
74 International Crisis Group, Crisis Group Update # 6 (28 February 2019), https://www.crisisgroup.org/middle-east-north-africa/gulf-and-arabian-peninsula/yemen/crisis-group-yemen-update-6 (accessed 29 January 2022).
75 Ibid.
76 International Crisis Group, Crisis Group Update # 10 (6 May 2019), https://www.crisisgroup.org/middle-east-north-africa/gulf-and-arabian-peninsula/yemen/crisis-group-yemen-update-10 (accessed 29 January 2022).
77 BBC Monitoring, "Yemen Rivals Intensify Battle for Key Central Province" (9 May 2019).
78 Vivian Lee, Yemen's Houthi Rebels Attack Saudi Oil Facilities, Escalating Tensions in Gulf, *The New York Times* (14 May 2019) https://www.nytimes.com/2019/05/14/world/middleeast/saudi-oil-attack.html (accessed 30 January 2020).
79 BBC Monitoring, "Saudi Coalition Says Air Strikes on Yemen Targets 'Legitimate'", SPA News Agency (16 May 2019).
80 Lee, "Yemen's Houthi Rebels Attack Saudi Oil Facilities, Escalating Tensions in Gulf".
81 Richard Roth, "Initial Findings on Gulf Tanker Attacks Point to 'State Actor' But Iran Not Mentioned by Name", *CNN* (7 June 2019), https://www.cnn.com/2019/06/06/middleeast/uae-saudi-oil-tankers-intl/index.html (accessed 2 February 2022).

82 Patrick Wintour, "Inquiry into Oil Tanker Stops Short of Blaming Iran", *The Guardian* (7 June 2019), https://www.theguardian.com/world/2019/jun/07/uae-tanker-attacks-un-iran-norway-saudi-arabia (accessed 2 February 2022).
83 AP, "Saudi Airport Struck by Deadly Attack", *The New York Times* (23 June 2019), https://www.nytimes.com/2019/06/23/world/middleeast/saudi-airport-attacked.html (accessed 2 February 2022); al-Jazeera, "Timeline: Hothis' Drone and Missile Attacks on Saudi Targets", *al-Jazeera* (14 September 2019), https://www.aljazeera.com/news/2019/9/14/timeline-houthis-drone-and-missile-attacks-on-saudi-targets (accessed 2 February 2022).
84 Ibid.
85 Yun Li, "Saudi Oil Production Cut by 50% after Drones Attack Crude Facilities", *CNBC* (14 September 2019), https://www.cnbc.com/2019/09/14/saudi-arabia-is-shutting-down-half-of-its-oil-production-after-drone-attack-wsj-says.html (accessed 5 February 2021).
86 Tweet by US Secretary of State, Mike Pompeo (14 September 2019), https://twitter.com/secpompeo/status/1172963090746548225 (accessed 6 February 2022).
87 https://www.reuters.com/article/us-saudi-aramco-attacks-iran-exclusive/exclusive-u-s-probe-of-saudi-oil-attack-shows-it-came-from-north-report-idUSKBN1YN299
88 France 24, "Weapons Used Against Saudi Arabia 'Were of Iranian Origin, UN Says", *France 24* (13 June 2020), https://www.france24.com/en/20200613-weapons-used-against-saudi-arabia-were-of-iranian-origin-un-says (accessed 5 February 2022).
89 Ibid.
90 David Hearst, "Exclusive: Yemen President Says UAE Acting Like Occupiers", *al-monitor* (12 May 2017), https://www.middleeasteye.net/news/exclusive-yemen-president-says-uae-acting-occupiers (accessed 8 January 2022).
91 Ibid.
92 MEE, "Yemenis March Against Hadi After Sacking Aden Governor", *Middle East Eye* (12 May 2017), https://www.middleeasteye.net/news/yemenis-march-against-hadi-after-sacking-aden-governor (accessed 9 February 2022).
93 Al-Jazeera, "GCC Rejects Formation of Yemen Transitional Council", *al-Jazeera* (13 May 2007), https://www.aljazeera.com/news/2017/5/13/gcc-rejects-formation-of-yemen-transitional-council (accessed 9 February 2022).
94 BBC Monitoring, "Southern Yemeni Separatists Threaten to Overthrow Government", Southern Transitional Website, BBC Monitoring (21 January 2018); AFP, "Many Dead in Yemen's Aden as PM Accuses Separatists of Coup" (28 January 2018), https://www.arabnews.com/node/1234541/middle-east (accessed 10 January 2022).
95 BBC Monitoring, "Clashes Resume in Yemen's Aden", *BBC Monitoring* (29 January 2018).
96 Another instance was when Transportation Minister, Saleh al-Jabwani, was unable to travel in the province of Shabwa when his delegation was stopped by the UAE-backed Shabwani Elite Forces and forced to return to Aden: BBC Monitoring, "Yemeni Minister Says UAE behind Decision to Restrict His Movements", Al-Mashhad al-Yemeni (26 February 2018).

97 BBC Monitoring, "Yemeni Security Director "Assassinated" in Aden", al-Masdat website (5 March 2018).
98 BBC Monitoring, "Al-Qaeda in Yemen Blames UAE for Assassination of Preachers" (20 April 2018).
99 Peter Salisbury, "Yemen's Southern Transitional Council: A Delicate Balancing Act", International Crisis Group (30 March 2021), https://www.crisisgroup.org/middle-east-north-africa/gulf-and-arabian-peninsula/yemen/yemens-southern-transitional-council-delicate-balancing-act (accessed 2 March 2022).
100 BBC Monitoring, "Resigning Yemen Minister Casts Critical Eye on Coalition", Facebook Post in Arabic (18 March 2018).
101 April Longley Alley, "Eight Days in Yemen - A Forgotten City in a Forgotten War", International Crisis Group (23 May 2018), https://www.crisisgroup.org/middle-east-north-africa/gulf-and-arabian-peninsula/yemen/eight-days-aden-forgotten-city-yemens-forgotten-war (accessed 12 February 2022).
102 Ibid.
103 International Crisis Group, "After Aden: Navigating Yemen's New Political Landscape" (30 August 2019), https://www.crisisgroup.org/middle-east-north-africa/gulf-and-arabian-peninsula/yemen/071-after-aden-navigating-yemens-new-political-landscape#:~:text=The%20latest%20political%20rupture%20came,of%20President%20Abed%20Rabbo%20Mansour (accessed 20 February 2022).
104 Ibid.
105 Aya Batrawy, "UAE Draws Down Troops in Yemen in 'Strategic Redeployment'", *ABC News* (8 July 2019), https://abcnews.go.com/International/wireStory/uae-draws-troops-yemen-strategic-redeployment-64200551 (accessed 20 February 2022).
106 Declan Walsh and David D. Kirkpatrick, "UAE Pulls Most Forces from Yemen in Blow to Saudi War Effort", *The New York Times* (11 July 2019), https://www.nytimes.com/2019/07/11/world/middleeast/yemen-emirates-saudi-war.html (accessed 22 February 2022).
107 Al-Jazeera, "Battle for Aden: Who Is Fighting Who and How Things Got Here", *al-Jazeera* (29 August 2019), https://www.aljazeera.com/news/2019/8/29/battle-for-aden-who-is-fighting-who-and-how-things-got-here (accessed 1 March 2022).
108 Aziz el-Yaakoubi, "Saudis Take Control of Yemen's Aden to End Stand-Off between Allies", *Reuters* (14 October 2019), https://www.reuters.com/article/us-yemen-security/saudis-take-control-of-yemens-aden-to-end-stand-off-between-allies-idUSKBN1WT19R (accessed 2 March 2022).
109 Ibrahim Jalal, "The Riyadh Agreement: Yemen's New Cabinet and What Remains to Be Done", *Middle East Eye* (1 February 2021), https://www.mei.edu/publications/riyadh-agreement-yemens-new-cabinet-and-what-remains-be-done (accessed 2 March 2022).
110 Ahmed Nagi, "Empowering the Separatists", Carnegie Middle East Center (9 July 2020), https://carnegie-mec.org/diwan/82263 (accessed 1 March 2022).
111 Ibid.
112 Reuters, "Yemen War: Separatists Declare Autonomous Rule in the South", *BBC News* (26 April 2020), https://www.bbc.com/news/world-middle-east-52428998 (accessed 2 March 2021).

113 Mohammed Mukhashaf, "Yemen Separatists Seize Remote Socotra Island from Saudi-Backed Government", *Reuters* (21 June 2020), https://www.reuters.com/article/us-yemen-security-separatists/yemen-separatists-seize-remote-socotra-island-from-saudi-backed-government-idUSKBN23S0DU (accessed 2 March 2022).
114 Jalal, "The Riyadh Agreement: Yemen's New Cabinet and What Remains to Be Done".
115 Nabil Abdullah al-Tamimi, "Yemeni and STC Forces Redeploy in Abyan, Aden", *al-Mashreq* (16 December 2020), https://almashareq.com/en_GB/articles/cnmi_am/features/2020/12/16/feature-02 (accessed 2 March 2022); Salisbury, "Yemen's Southern Transitional Council: A Delicate Balancing Act".
116 Joseph Stepansky, "Timeline of Trump's Shifting Justifications for Soleimani Killing", *al-Jazeera* (19 February 2020) https://www.aljazeera.com/news/2020/2/19/timeline-of-trumps-shifting-justifications-for-soleimani-killing (accessed 12 March 2022).
117 John Hudson, Miss Ryan, and Josh Dawsey, "On the Day U.S. Forces Killed Soleimani, They Targeted a Senior Iranian Official in Yemen", *The Washington Post* (10 January 2020), https://www.washingtonpost.com/world/national-security/on-the-day-us-forces-killed-soleimani-they-launched-another-secret-operation-targeting-a-senior-iranian-official-in-yemen/2020/01/10/60f86dbc-3245-11ea-898f-eb846b7e9feb_story.html (accessed 12 March 2022).
118 A Houthi-run outlet quoted protester chanting "killing two Muslim leaders amounts to a blatant aggression against the entire Umma [Muslim nation], which compels Muslims to shoulder their responsibilities and to face off an enemy who targets them all without exception", BBC Monitoring *Al-Masirah TV* (6 January 2020).
119 Bethan McKernan, "Yemen: Death Toll Rises to 116 from Suspected Houthi Missile Attack", *The Guardian* (21 January 2020), https://www.theguardian.com/world/2020/jan/21/yemen-death-toll-rises-houthi-missile-attack-government-forces (accessed 12 March 2022).
120 International Crisis Group, March 2020 Alerts, https://www.crisisgroup.org/crisiswatch/march-alerts-and-february-trends-2020 (accessed 12 March 2022).
121 Ibid.
122 Al Jazeera, "Officials Say Yemen's Rebel Seize Strategic Northern City", *al Jazeera* (1 March 2020) https://www.aljazeera.com/news/2020/3/1/officials-say-yemens-rebels-seize-strategic-northern-city (accessed 28 March 2022).
123 MEE Correspondent, "In Dramatic Counterattack, Houthis Take Yemen's Al-Jawf and Eye Marib", *Middle East Eye* (2 March 2020), https://www.middleeasteye.net/news/dramatic-counterattack-houthis-take-yemens-al-jawf-and-eyemarib (accessed 12 March 2022).
124 Ibid.
125 UN News, "COVID-19 in Yemen: Saudi Coalition Ceasefire Declared in Bid to Contain Coronavirus", United Nations (9 April 2020), https://news.un.org/en/story/2020/04/1061422 (accessed 29 March 2021).
126 Office of the Special Envoy of the Secretary-General for Yemen, Statement by the Special Envoy or Yemen on the unilateral ceasefire by

the Joint Forces Command (8 April 2020), https://osesgy.unmissions.org/statement-special-envoy-yemen-unilateral-ceasefire-joint-forces-command (accessed 29 March 2022); Reuters, Covid Tracker – Yemen, https://graphics.reuters.com/world-coronavirus-tracker-and-maps/countries-and-territories/yemen/ (accessed 29 March 2022).
127 Cathrin Schaer, "COVID-19 Vaccines as 'Biological Warfare' in Middle East?", *DW* (5 February 2021), https://www.dw.com/en/covid-vaccines-as-passive-biological-warfare-in-middle-east/a-56471435 (accessed 29 March 2022).
128 Ibid.
129 Reuters, "War and Doubts Slow COVID-19 Vaccination in Disputed Yemen City", *Reuters* (3 May 2021), https://www.reuters.com/world/middle-east/war-doubts-slow-covid-19-vaccination-disputed-yemen-city-2021-05-03/ (accessed 29 March 2022).
130 International Crisis Group, Crisis Watch November–December 2020, https://www.crisisgroup.org/crisiswatch/crisiswatch-december-alerts-and-november-trends-2020 (accessed 29 March 2022).
131 Ibid.
132 Al-Jazeera, "Yemen: Houthis Claim Killing of Several Saudi Soldiers in Marib", *al-Jazeera* (30 November 2020), https://www.aljazeera.com/news/2020/11/30/houthis-claim-killing-of-several-saudi-soldiers-in-marib (accessed 29 March 2022).
133 UN Press Release, Welcoming Mass Prisoner Swap in Yemen as 'Airlift of Hope', Speakers Urge Government, Houthi Rebels to Negotiate Durable Peace, during Security Council Briefing SC/14328, https://www.un.org/press/en/2020/sc14328.doc.htm (accessed 1 April 2022); al-Jazeera, "Yemen's Houthis Hit Saudi Aramco Site in Jeddah" (23 November 2020), https://www.aljazeera.com/news/2020/11/23/yemens-houthis-say-they-fired-missile-at-saudi-aramco-site (accessed 1 April 2022).
134 Al-Jazeera, "New Yemen Gov't Sworn in after Saudi-Brokered Power-Sharing Deal" (26 December 2020), https://www.aljazeera.com/news/2020/12/26/yemens-new-government-sworn-in-after-power-sharing-agreement (accessed 1 April 2022).
135 UN News, "UN Chief and Yemen Envoy Condemn Deadly Aden Airport Attack" (30 December 2020), https://news.un.org/en/story/2020/12/1081132 (accessed 1 April 2022).
136 France 24, "UN Report Points to Huthis for December Attack on Aden Airport", *France 24* (31 March 2021), https://www.france24.com/en/live-news/20210331-un-report-points-to-huthis-for-december-attack-on-aden-airport (accessed 1 April 2022).
137 Ibid.
138 UN News, "UN Officials Fear US Terrorist Designation Will Hasten Famine in Yemen" (14 January 2021), https://news.un.org/en/story/2021/01/1082082 (accessed 4 April 2022).
139 Anthiny Bliken, Secretary of State, Revocation of the Terrorist Deisginations of Ansarallah (12 February 2021), https://www.state.gov/revocation-of-the-terrorist-designations-of-ansarallah/ (accessed 5 April 2022).
140 Ibid.
141 Jonathan Landay and Jarret Renshaw, "Biden Ends U.S. Support for Saudi Arabia in Yemen, Says War 'Has to End'", *Reuters* (4 February

2021), https://www.reuters.com/article/usa-biden-yemen-int/biden-ends-u-s-support-for-saudi-arabia-in-yemen-says-war-has-to-end-idUSKBN2A4268 (accessed 6 April 2022); the deal included 280 AIM-120C-7/C-8 Advanced Medium Range Air-to-Air Missiles (AMRAAM), 596 LAU-128 Missile Rail Launchers (MRL) along with containers and support equipment, spare parts, U.S. Government and contractor engineering and technical support.

142 Ibid.
143 Isabel Debre, "Saudi TV: Yemen Rebel Attack on Airport Sets Plane on Fire", Associated Press (10 February 2021), https://apnews.com/article/middle-east-yemen-dubai-saudi-arabia-united-arab-emirates-a351ca2f95c68ebf08c385742deef2ac (accessed 9 April 2022).
144 Andrew Desiderio, "Senate Backs Biden Admin Weapons Sale to Saudi Arabia", *Politico* (7 December 2021), https://www.politico.com/news/2021/12/07/senate-biden-saudi-arabia-523915 (accessed 6 April 2022).
145 al-Arabiya, "Arab Coalition Destroys Houthi Missile Launchers in Yemen's Marib: SPA", *al-Arabiya* (11 March 2021), https://english.alarabiya.net/News/gulf/2021/03/11/Arab-Coalition-destroys-Houthi-missile-launcher-in-Yemen-s-Marib-SPA /(accessed 9 April 2022).
146 See Tweet by Saudi Ministry of Foreign Affairs (22 March 2021), https://twitter.com/KSAmofaEN/status/1374047978583908361 (accessed 9 April 2022).
147 Marc Daou, "Why Yemen's Houthis Turned Down Saudi Arabia's Ceasefire Offer", *France 24* (24 March 2021), https://www.france24.com/en/middle-east/20210324-why-yemen-s-houthis-turned-down-saudi-arabia-s-ceasefire-offer (accessed 9 April 2022).
148 Ibid.
149 Ibid.
150 Jon Gambrell, "Saudi-Offered, Rebel-Rejected Cease-Fire Starts in Yemen War", *The Washington Post* (30 March 2021), https://www.washingtonpost.com/world/gulf-states-plan-yemen-talks-without-houthi-rebels-present/2022/03/29/3bfa7fc0-af23-11ec-9dbd-0d4609d44c1c_story.html (accessed 9 April 2022).
151 Crisis Group, Briefing Np 84/Middle East and North Africa, After al-Bayda, the Beginning of the Endgame for Northern Yemen?" (14 October 2021), https://www.crisisgroup.org/middle-east-north-africa/gulf-and-arabian-peninsula/yemen/b84-after-al-bayda-beginning-endgame-northern-yemen (accessed 9 April 2022).
152 Governorates are stacked in the same order, based on total reported fatalities throughout the conflict, to facilitate interpretation. Roughly half of Yemeni Governorates are aggregated together and represented by the top band. These governorates experienced relatively less violence than others and would not be discernable separately.

5 External Patrons of Surrogates in Yemen's Civil War

On April 7, 2022, the Saudi Crown Prince delivered to President Hadi a decree that surrendered his presidential powers and confined him to his residence-in-exile in Riyadh indefinitely.[1] Throughout the war, Hadi and his ministers had moved between Yemen, Saudi Arabia, and UAE, attempting to govern in exile. As a result, the Yemeni president and his administration lacked legitimacy inside Yemen. This move by Saudi Arabia's leadership—stripping a foreign head of state of their jurisdiction over their country—showed the extent of Saudi's control over political affairs in Yemen.

Unlike the conflicts in Iraq and Afghanistan during which Western powers were central belligerents, the conflicts in Libya, Syria, and Yemen were proxy conflicts. The US and European governments were almost entirely indirectly engaged, and with the exception of the resulting Syrian refugee crisis, Western media largely framed these conflicts as regional civil wars rather than proxy wars with Western involvement. American leaders especially knew there was not domestic support for US involvement in another ground war in the Middle East. In the case of Yemen, the overriding narrative was one of "sectarian warfare" triggered and maintained by Saudi-Iranian rivalry and inherent Sunni-Shi'a divide.

This chapter analyzes the main external patrons—Iran, Saudi Arabia, and the United Arab Emirates—and analyzes their respective strategies during the conflict. We term the United States a "super patron" due to the two-level proxy system it employed in pursuit of its larger strategic interests in the Middle East. The US special forces worked directly with proxies in Yemen, providing training and logistical support to aid in their fight against Houthis and by extension, their Iranian patrons. But the United States also used Saudi Arabia as a proxy, who itself was using pro-Hadi forces in Yemen as proxies, as a means to expand capabilities of the anti-Houthi forces while maintaining distance from the war and deniability about its own involvement. In essence, the United States was

DOI: 10.4324/9781003262602-5

employing proxies in Saudi Arabia and in Yemen as means to off-shore balance against Iran. Despite its super patron role, and although it was sometimes able to shape the Saudi-led coalition at key moments (e.g., restraining the UAE from conducting a ground offensive to capture Hodeidah, help brokering the 2018 Stockholm Agreement), it was largely unable to exert meaningful pressure on Saudi Arabia, the UAE, and Qatar and failed to help the coalition a military victory, nor was it even able to broker a negotiated settlement.[2]

As the war progressed, fissures between Saudi Arabia and the UAE over war goals, respective national interests, and strategies resulted in support of opposing proxies in Yemen which would ultimately prolong the conflict to the detriment of Yemen's population. Moreover, the complexity of the civil war and the broader geostrategic context of the region permitted different patrons to choose between multiple proxies across the region. As the cohesion of the coalition eroded as coalition members worked toward their own interests through their own chosen proxies, major disputes prompted the breakdown of diplomatic relations between Qatar on one side and Saudi Arabia and the UAE on the other side from 2017 through 2021. These major fissures, exacerbated by the US government's inability to effectively reign in its own proxies despite its super patron role, helped the Iranian government to sustain a "bait and bleed" strategy which not only drained the Gulf monarchies' resources but also denied the Saudi-led coalition to the ability decisively dominate the military balance and ultimately achieve a political victory.

Patrons' political systems are central to their decision-making during proxy war.[3] Non-democracies such as Saudi Arabia, UAE, Qatar, and Iran are less constrained by domestic scrutiny over alleged war crimes and other domestically unpalatable behaviors, although they still had to cater to domestic audiences about the merits of prolonged interventions and casualties of their own armed forces. On the other hand, as a democracy the US government faced far more domestic backlash over its policy in Yemen and toward Saudi Arabia, especially when US patronage could be directly connected to civilian victimization. On the other hand, although previous US engagements in the Middle East had been domestically framed as benevolent interventions in civil wars, the assassination of Jamal Khashoggi by Saudi operatives refocused domestic attention inside the United States toward its support for the Saudi Regime and the regime's willingness to callously pursue its objectives without regard for civilian wellbeing. Once the American public began connecting and condemning the United States' military support to Saudi Arabia over the kingdom's negligent and ostensibly intentional civilian targeting, Congress invoked the War Powers Resolution in 2019 to interrupt the United States' patronage of the conflict. This was historic as it was only the second time since the inception of the War Powers Act in 1973 that it was used. It was also a rare bipartisan rebuke of US President Donald Trump's foreign policy. While President Trump eventually vetoed the measure, which demanded an end to US involvement in the war, it marked an important reproach of US support for a proxy that stood accused of war crimes and crimes against humanity and signaled wavering American resolve vis-à-vis coalition patronage.[4] While this effectively "burnt" Saudi Arabia as an intermediate proxy for US ambitions, the Saudi-UAE fissure enabled the United States to maintain its engagement using the UAE as a less visible branch of the conflict network. Weapons transfers from the United States to Saudi Arabia halted. Between April 2018 and May 2019, the US Defense Security Cooperation Agency, responsible for reviewing and approving sales of military equipment to foreign powers and submitting those reports to congress for oversight, did not greenlight any sales to either Saudi Arabia or the UAE. While it would authorize sales to both countries in May 2019, it was not until December 2020, just one month before President Trump would leave office, that the DSCA would authorize another sale to the kingdom. During that same period, sales to UAE totaling nearly $25 billion were approved.[5] Upon taking office, President Biden's decision to halt US support for Saudi war efforts in 2021, followed by his visit to mend relations following the global surge of gas prices in 2022, has to be seen within this context.[6]

Saudi Arabia and United Arab Emirates

Saudi motivations for the intervention ultimately have to be seen within the historical context and Riyadh's history of interference in and control over Yemeni politics. According to a Yemeni politician, Saudi rulers sought two outcomes from the war. First, for Yemen was to be fully dependent on Saudi Arabia, with all political decisions dominated by Riyadh. Second, they sought to replicate the "Bahrain Model" for Yemen's foreign affairs, where Yemen would be fully aligned with Saudi foreign policy. Yemen would ultimately become a Saudi vassal state.[7] Another primary variable for Riyadh was energy security. Saudi Arabia's proposed al-Mahra pipeline would traverse Yemen's al-Mahra governorate, effectively circumventing the Bab al-Mandab Strait or the Strait of Hormuz. By 2019, the Saudi had over a dozen military bases with thousands of troops in the al-Mahra governorate while assuming control the governorate's airport, border crossings, and main seaport.[8]

As far as US officials were concerned, Saudis had failed by not considering the extended impact of their intervention. The Saudi leadership's risk calculus has always been very short term orientated around a confidence that their sophisticated, US-procured military equipment would easily bring about their political objectives. According to a US official in the Department of State, nobody in Riyadh expected a proxy war when they launched the military campaign. What was meant to be a quick military intervention to reinstate the allied Yemeni government became an existential threat from Saudi's vantage point. Not only had the war effort claimed substantial resources, Saudis started to face ballistic missiles fired from Yemeni into Saudi territory and the very real prospect of an Iranian proxy state on its southern border.

Throughout the war, it became evident to Yemen's political establishment that Saudi rulers would only accept a fully independent Yemen with assurances that it would not pose any threats to Saudi security. This would include a scenario where Yemen would indefinitely remain weak. One Yemeni politician remarked that Saudis would only end the war if they found a governing model for Yemen that had the "right chemistry for Saudi Arabia".[9] From the perspective of US forces inside Yemen, however, Saudi leadership lacked both the strategy and the military skill to prevail, failing to translate their formidable firepower into any meaningful coercive statecraft. Saudi bombings were primarily meant to disrupt Iranian-Houthi smuggling networks viewed as existential threat, but instead created a humanitarian crisis.[10]

The lack of a coherent strategy condemned the Saudi coalition to become bogged down in the conduct of war without a clear roadmap toward a viable political outcome. Saudi operational incompetence only compounded the lack of statesmanship that could have pushed for a political settlement. As observed by US forces on the ground, the Saudi military's lack of tactical and operational warfare capabilities prevented them from decisively shifting the military balance in the Yemeni government's favor despite their superior firepower. The country commands a high-tech military that is almost entirely underwritten by US weapons exports, and for a military intervention to succeed, in particular one that is primarily fought from the air, operational and tactical proficiency is paramount. In the Saudi military, most high-ranking officers received their positions through entitlement rather than merit. Throughout the ranks, officers lack training in both conventional and special operations warfare, leaving them ill-suited to translate their US-procured firepower into either battlefield or political gains.[11] They also faced a formidable enemy in Iran. The Islamic Revolutionary Guard Corps, then under the leadership of General

Qasem Soleimani, honed their superior asymmetrical warfare capabilities and experience in the Yemeni conflict. By the time Saudi intervened in Yemen in order to balance against Tehran, the Iranian government had already been effectively projecting military and soft power across the region into Iraq, Lebanon, and Syria for decades. Iran had not only the experience and domestically sourced military hardware but also the political will and requisite skillsets to effectively execute special military operations. Saudi Arabia was unable to match, never mind balance against Iranian power in Yemen on its own.[12]

Saudi military incompetence mandated military assistance from the US government. Acting as the super patron, American interests aligned with Saudi Arabia's in that the defeat of the Houthis and the reinstatement of the Hadi government would weaken Iranian influence in the country and region. However, the US government was also mindful of appearing complicit with Saudi forces' misconduct and the numerous allegations of human rights violations and war crimes. According to US officials in the Department of Defense and Department of State, "the Saudis whitewashed an American-sponsored initiative to investigate errant airstrikes and often ignored a voluminous no-strike list".[13] Faced with blatant disregard for US military advice, former Assistant Secretary of State Tom Malinowski stated that:

> In the end, we concluded that they were just not willing to listen … They were given specific coordinates of targets that should not be struck and they continued to strike them. That struck me as a willful disregard of advice they were getting.[14]

In an effort to keep Saudi military attacks in Yemen within the boundaries of international humanitarian law while also helping the Saudi to actually win the war, US military assistance to Saudi Arabia included flight training, technical training, professional military education, and specialized training contracted through the US Air Force and other DoD agencies.[15] This particular assistance program by the US military was approved by the US Defense Security Cooperation Agency in 2017 and constituted a $750 million training for the Royal Saudi Air Force focusing on "civilian casualty avoidance, the law of armed conflict, human rights command and control, and targeting via MTT [Mobile Training Teams] and/or broader Programs of Instruction (POIs)".[16] By 2018, nearly 100 US military personnel were advising or assisting the Saudi war effort, 35 of which were based inside Saudi Arabia.[17] Notwithstanding these efforts, US military officials that were assigned to the coalition's war room in Riyadh observed that "inexperienced Saudi pilots flew at high altitudes to avoid enemy fire"

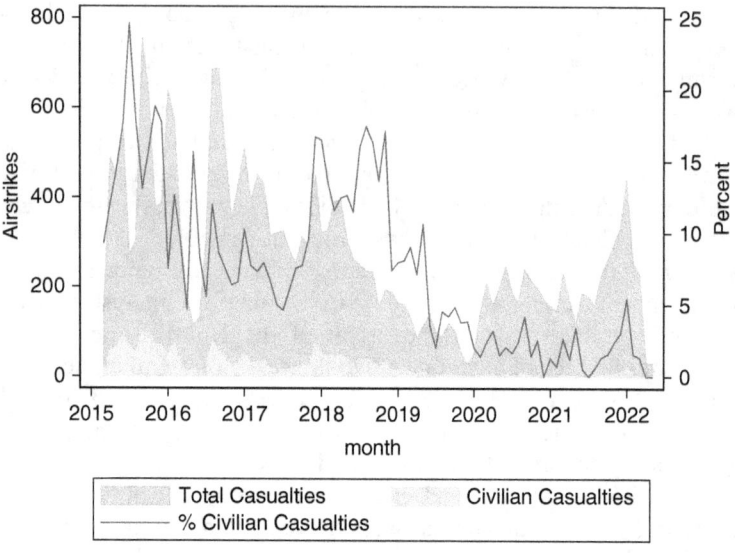

Figure 5.1 Coalition Air Strikes and Civilian Casualties.

which "reduced the risk to the pilots but transferred it to civilians, who were exposed to less accurate bombings".[18] Coalition military planners also allegedly "misidentified targets and their pilots struck them at the wrong time—destroying a vehicle as it passed through a crowded bazaar, for instance, instead of waiting until it reached an open road". US military observed noted that the Saudi coalition almost always ignored the no-strike list provided by US Central Command and the UN.[19] Of the 23,712 coalition air strikes launched since 2015, 2,134 air strikes—a staggering 9%—are reported by ACLED to have involved civilian targets as either the primary or collateral target (Figure 5.1). Coalition air strikes also blanketed the western governorates, striking nearly all population centers within Yemen's most densely populated governorates at some point during the conflict's progression (Figure 5.2).[20] Civilians were fair game to Saudi pilots and the top brass in general and there were very few locations within Yemen where civilians could seek refuge without risk of an errant strike.

Saudi and UAE Control over the Government of Yemen

Between 2014 and 2022 when the Saudi leadership eventually deposed Hadi as president of Yemen, Hadi and his cabinet governed at the mercy

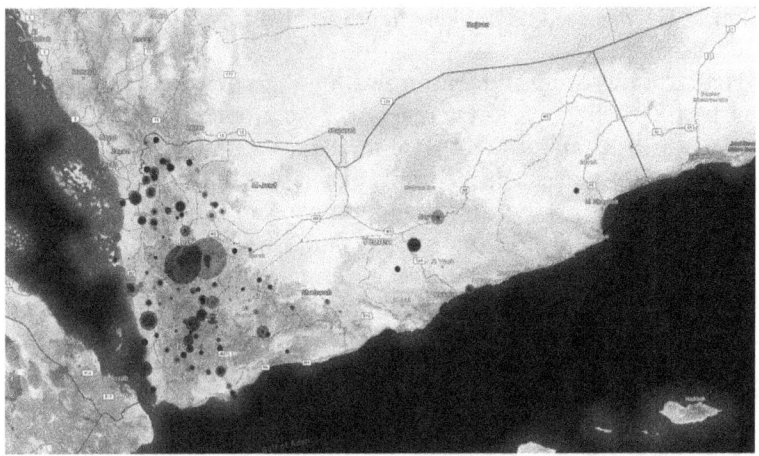

Figure 5.2 Civilian Casualties from SLC Air Strikes, 2015–2020.

of Saudi Arabia and the UAE. Since Saudi Arabia sought to make Yemen a permanent vassal state of Saudi Arabia, Yemen's government in exile not only lacked autonomy in decision-making and governance but also legitimacy. The entire process of appointing of cabinet ministers and other government officials including ambassadors was subject to Saudi influence. Since Hadi and all of his cabinet ministers resided in Riyadh or Dubai throughout most of the war, the Yemeni bureaucracy inside government-controlled Yemeni territory, mostly confined to Aden, was left to administer day to day governmental operations on their own. As recounted by a Yemeni government insider, ministries and government offices were effectively running themselves. For example, the police and the Department of Immigration and Passports continued working even though the Minister of Interior never resided in Aden. The Customs Department, Tax Department, and Ports were operational even though the Ministers of Finance and Commerce were hardly presiding over their respective portfolios.[21] It was at the discretion of the Saudi and UAE governments respectively to permit the Yemeni President and cabinet ministers to return to Yemen on certain occasions. Ministers including Prime Minister Maeen Abdulmalik Saeed never remained in Aden for more than one month. While the Riyadh Agreement stipulated for the cabinet to return to Aden for visits, leaders in Riyadh and Dubai only permitted these sporadic visits to the capital because the Prime Minister was never considered a political threat to Saudi interests. Saeed was a 45-year-old young technocrat who lacked a political legacy or any real tribal and military leverage in Yemeni politics. He was seen as unlikely figure to challenge or undermine the Saudi's agenda.[22]

Hadi too was confined to govern within the parameters provided to him by the coalition, and the reality on the ground in the Aden was that it was STC militias that were in charge of security. While UAE was restricting movement of Hadi's cabinet to and from Aden, STC militias were able to exert more and more local control in the capital. STC militias controlled the streets and the military and police forces in Aden, while more general governmental agencies tasked with public administration (the Central Bank, Department of Education, Department of Finance) were run by Hadi government technocrats. These parallel and competing governing bodies in the capital put residents in a difficult position. While residents understood that true authority lied with the STC and by extension with the UAE, they maneuvered carefully, attempting to be compliant with orders from both the Hadi government as well as the STC. For example, the import-reliant business community was asked reduce their customs and tariff dues owed to the Hadi government by 20% and instead pay that sum to the STC Security Belt forces which by 2018 had become the de facto police in the south.[23] Security Belt and UAE forces controlled most everything in Aden. Even Hadi himself was unable to move freely. During one of his visits to the capital in 2018, the senior UAE military commander would not permit Hadi to leave his residence, confining him to the Maashiq Presidential Palace; it was only with Saudi intervention that a major violent clash between UAE forces and Hadi's guards were prevented.[24]

The UAE's relationship to the Hadi government was undermined by its own objectives. As far as Yemenis were concerned, UAE goals in Yemen were primarily driven by their own geopolitical ambitions to project power across the region. The Yemeni government perceived the Emirates as bent on dominating and controlling all of Yemen. To that end, UAE never saw Hadi as a partner but rather someone who had to be saved politically and propped up by the coalition. It was an act of rescue instead of an exercise among equals. It was evident to Yemeni government officials that the UAE saw itself as "Hadi's savior". The Emirates also believed that it was justified in dominating Yemeni affairs given all the resources they had spent on the war effort and political engineering and the impact it had on its own reputation and tourism.[25] Against this stood Hadi and his government which according to Yemeni government insiders, saw themselves as the ruling class of the country and that the UAE's role was nothing more than temporary assistance.[26]

Throughout the conflict, UAE forces were accused of maintaining secret detention centers by the United Nations. A 2018 report to the UN Security Council of the Panel of Experts on Yemen stated:

The forces of the United Arab Emirates were responsible for:

i   torture (including beatings, electrocution, constrained suspension and imprisonment in a metal cell ('the cage') in the sun);
ii   ill treatment;
iii   denial of timely medical treatment;
iv   denial of due process rights; and
v   enforced disappearance of detainees, in violation of international humanitarian law and international human rights law.[27]

Neither Saudi Arabia nor the UAE sought an independent Yemen. Instead, each pursued their own visions of Yemen's political future, incompatible with the other's and therefore impossible to maintain in the long run.

In operational and tactical terms, Saudi-UAE divisions also undermined the coalition's overall military objectives. As observed by one member of the US military in a small Forward Operating Base in Makala, Saudi and Emirati forces were always competing for control and power on the ground.[28] While UAE forces were battlefield commanders on the ground, Saudi forces were embedded within the Yemeni coastguard to safeguard the coastline and disrupt smuggling. Saudi Arabia largely bankrolled Yemeni forces and also paid tribal elders keep road checkpoints across central Yemen staffed. Unlike UAE forces working directly with locals on the ground, the Saudis opted to pay their local proxies. As observed by the US military, a major challenge of this approach was the timely paying of salaries, which were often not paid on time and in some instances, not at all. With tribes effectively acting as mercenaries, opportunities arose for ISIS and AQAP to buy tribal loyalties through monthly or daily salaries. Several militias that were initially bankrolled by Saudi Arabia went unpaid for stretches of up to six months. Many of these switched sides, now working for AQAP purely on financial grounds.[29] To the US forces stationed in Yemen in order to destroy AQAP, it was evident that unlike Iraq or Syria where political fault lines were determined ideological and/or sectarian ties, the main motivator in Yemen was the need for money and other resources in light of the dire humanitarian crisis and the inability of the failed central government to meet even the most basic human needs.[30] By all accounts, Saudi and

UAE divisions coupled with the lack of effective Saudi strategy for the country jeopardized the patrons' control over their proxies.

United States

US foreign policy toward the war in Yemen had spanned three US presidents, from Barack Obama to Donald Trump to Joe Biden. The most comprehensive explanation of why the Obama administration supported Saudi Arabia came in the form of an open letter by 30 former senior US officials on November 11, 2018 including Obama's National Security Adviser Susan E. Rice, CIA director John Brennan, and Deputy Secretary of State Tony Blinken (who would go on to serve as Secretary of State for the Biden administration). Intended as a rebuke of the Trump administration's unconditional support for Saudi Arabia, the joint statement read that "the Obama administration provided some intelligence, refueling, and logistical assistance to the Saudi-led coalition, in response to a legitimate threat posed by missiles on the Saudi border and the Houthi overthrow of the Yemeni government, with support from Iran". The letter further noted that the Obama administration's support was meant as an "effort to gain leverage to push the coalition to abide by international humanitarian law and support parallel diplomatic efforts", but conceded that this approach did "not succeed in limiting and ultimately ending the war".[31] The signatories tried to frame the Obama administration's policy toward Saudi Arabia as more "conditional", saying that they had not intended for "US support to become a blank check" and called on the Trump administration to end US involvement in the war.[32] The letter strongly criticized Secretary Pompeo for formally announcing that Trump administration "would continue to support the coalition in light of 'demonstrable actions to reduce the risk of harm to civilians … resulting from military operations …'". The Obama-era national security officials criticized Pompeo for the decision and for overruling professionals in the State Department.[33] Notwithstanding the revisionist nature of the letter, President Obama's support for Saudi Arabia reflected two foreign policy determinants: first, it sought to reassure Saudi Arabia of the alliance with the United States following the Nuclear Deal with Iran; and second, as Iran's role in Yemen started to impact the military balance, US support was a means to help balance against Iranian power. Much like the Reagan administration's support for Saddam Hussein during the Iran-Iraq War, US military and political support for Riyadh had all the trimmings of off-shore balancing. However, because of the lack of effective Saudi strategy and failure to reshape Yemeni politics according to their national security priorities as well as Houthi battleground gains, it was evident to US officials early on into the conflict that a quick Saudi victory was unlikely.

Human Rights Watch called the letter an incomplete reckoning by Obama administration officials and noted that:

> The Obama administration, not learning enough from past foreign military experiences in Yemen, accepted baseless assurances from the Saudis—including the then-deputy Crown Prince Mohamed Bin Salman and the inexperienced Saudi military—that they would overthrow the Houthis in months. The US decidedly looked the other way from Saleh's strong support for the Houthis, including vast stores of weaponry from the Defense Ministry, an institution that remained loyal to Saleh. The war dragged on, with limited military gains by the Saudi-led coalition, but a rising toll of unnecessary and unlawful death and destruction.[34]

With Yemen having been classified a safe haven for terrorists by the US Department of State, the Obama administration deployed US Special Operations forces in to fight AQAP in the country. Although the US government had engagements in Yemen since 2002 following the 9/11 attacks, under the Obama administration the objective in Yemen was expanded to not only disrupt and destroy AQAP but also to provide training to the Yemeni government that would permit them to act as a partner in counter-terrorism.[35] When AQAP's leader in Yemen, Anwar al-Awlaki (who was also an American citizen) was killed by a US drone strike in September 2011, President Obama stated that he would not "hesitate to use force to protect our nation, including from the threat of terrorism".[36] The Obama administration alone would authorize a minimum of 162 drone strikes in Yemen between January 2009 and December 2016, killing at least 801 people (including 131 civilians and 34 children).[37] With the emergence of ISIS in the Middle East in 2014, US Special Operations forces continued with counter-terrorism operations in Yemen that were maintained by both the Trump and Biden administrations.[38] As much as the United States acted as super patron in the conflict to balance against Iran, US national security priorities still compelled the US government to remain an active belligerent in the Yemeni theater against ISIS while using proxies to support anti-Houthi campaigns. The 2018 National Defense Strategy in particular laid out these objectives, dubbing China, Russia, and Iran "practitioners of campaigns of disinformation, deception, sabotage, and economic coercion, as well as proxy, guerrilla, and covert operations". The Irregular Warfare Annex of the document called for the US military to engage in "proactive, dynamic, and unorthodox approaches to [irregular warfare] that can shape, prevent, and prevail against our nation's adversaries".[39] To all three US administrations, Yemen represented not just a theater in which the US military presence was required for counter-terrorism operations against direct threaten US national security but also a battleground to "bait and bleed" Iran by means of offshore balancing via proxies.

Donald Trump's first officials overseas trip as president was to Saudi Arabia. Saudi Arabia was an atypical destination for a new president's first overseas trip. With the exception of Richard Nixon, all US presidents since John F. Kennedy had begun their overseas state visits in either Canada, Mexico, or the United Kingdom; Nixon's first visit was Belgium, with the United Kingdom his second stop on the trip. This stark deviation from what the diplomatic corps considered American tradition sent a strong message to Riyadh and the UAE, both of which felt emboldened by this gesture.[40] Trump framed his visit as a way to combat terrorism and together with King Salman and Egyptian President Abdel Fattha el-Sissi inaugurated the Global Center for Combatting Extremist Ideology in Riyadh. This visit would set the overall tone for US foreign policy toward Saudi Arabia under the Trump administration. His entire term was marked by unconditional support for Saudi Arabia and what became known as the "maximum pressure campaign" against Iran. When President Trump unilaterally withdrew from the nuclear agreement with Iran in 2018 and designated Iran's Revolutionary Guard Corps as foreign terrorist organization, it was as much as a reflection of Israeli priorities (President Trump's second state visit, just following Saudi Arabia) as it was a reset of US-Saudi relations.[41] Both Israelis and Saudis had felt abandoned after Obama's diplomatic engagement with Iran and President Trump was eager to mend relations.

Although the Trump administration's unconditional support for Saudi rulers may not appear on the surface a continuation of previous administration's policies, it is evident that personal business interests weighed heavily on US-Saudi bilateral relations. Trump's son in law and key adviser Jared Kushner and Secretary of the Treasury Steven Mnuchin were at the center on all decisions on Saudi Arabia. During their first six months after leaving the White House, Kushner and Mnuchin would receive over $4.5 billion in Saudi investments.[42] President Trump also secretly authorized the deployment of the US Army's Special Forces, the Green Berets, in December 2017 after ballistic missiles launched from Yemen came close to the Saudi capital.

Crown Prince Mohammed bin Salman had reportedly renewed his longstanding request that the United States send troops to help Saudi defense against Houthis.[43] The Green Berets trained Saudi ground troops to secure their border while US intelligence analysts provided Saudi border forces assistance in locating Houthi missile sites within Yemen. Along the entire Saudi-Yemeni border, US commandos were employing surveillance to gather electronic signals which enabled the tracking of Houthi weapons and launch sites.[44] When the mission was eventually disclosed to the public, US Senator Tim Kaine (D-VA), a member of the Armed Services Committee, called the Green Berets mission a "purposeful blurring of lines between train and equip missions and combat".[45]

Qatar Blockade

In 2017, Saudi Arabia, the UAE, Bahrain, and Egypt imposed an embargo on Qatar over its alleged support for Hamas, the Muslim Brotherhood, and its developing ties to Iran. The embargo would last through 2021 when diplomatic relations were re-established following mediation by Kuwait. President Trump sided with the quartet even though cutting off air, sea, and diplomatic relations with Doha not only jeopardized their own efforts in Yemen but also ultimately conflicted with official US foreign policy toward Qatar. Not unlike Trump's parallel diplomacy toward Ukraine—which ultimately lead to his first impeachment—then Secretary of State Rex Tillerson, charged with mediating discussions between Qatar and Saudi Arabia, was blindsided when in a tweet, Trump took credit for the blockade.[46] In a 2019 testimony before the House committee on Foreign Affairs, Tillerson testified that Jared Kushner had engaged foreign leaders independently, on behalf of the United States' government, without coordinating with the Department of State. Tillerson was effectively shut out of meetings and policy deliberations that would normally fall under his purview as Secretary of State. Tillerson and the then Defense Secretary James Mattis were caught completely off guard by Kushner having advance knowledge of the blockade on Qatar.[47] In fact, both secretaries were in Australia when they learned about the severing of relations between Qatar and the US's other Middle Eastern allies.

The Qataris had committed only a small contingent of forces in Yemen, about 1,000 in total. On June 8, 2017, Qatar was formally expelled from the coalition.[48] Underestimating Qatari resilience, the quartet not only failed to reign in Doha's independent foreign policy but also ultimately helped boost its economic independence and diversification.⁴⁹ Most importantly, far from containing Doha's diplomatic outreach to Tehran, bilateral ties instead expanded as a result of the blockade.⁵⁰ Not only did the Qatar crisis undermine coalition efforts in Yemen, but again Saudi coercive diplomacy proved unable to force a reversal of Doha's foreign policy. As far as the super patron was concerned, American policy toward the quartet and Qatar did not reflect American strategic interests in either Qatar or the broader region. Rather, they almost entirely mirrored Saudi interests. While Saudi Arabia failed to change Qatari behavior, the United States seemed either unable to unwilling influence Saudi rulers during the crisis.

The Khashoggi Murder and the War Powers Resolution on Yemen

The murder of Saudi dissident and Washington Post journalist Jamal Khashoggi by Saudi government agents in the Saudi consulate in Istanbul on October 2, 2018 would cast a shadow on US-Saudi relations and ultimately lead to a congressional censure of Riyadh's war in Yemen. Trump's continued defense of Saudi Crown Prince Mohammed bin Salman despite the determination by the US intelligence community that he had ordered the gruesome murder was enough to prompt Trump loyalists and pro-Saudi Republican senators to break with the president and openly questioned US support for Saudi's war effort in Yemen. US Senator Lindsay Graham (R-SC) said he felt "betrayed by Saudi Arabia" adding that "the relationship is important, but our values are more important".⁵¹ The Senate Resolution on Yemen, S.J.Res.7, was introduced by US Senator Bernie Sanders (I-VT) on January 30, 2019 and directed "the removal of United States Armed Forces from hostilities in the Republic of Yemen that have not been authorized by Congress". While the resolution excluded US forces that were "engaged in operations against al Qaeda", the bill specifically defined hostilities to include "in-flight refueling of non-United States aircraft conducting missions as part of the ongoing civil war in Yemen".⁵² Essentially, the resolution called the US government to suspend all support for Saudi Arabia's war efforts. Although the resolution would be vetoed by Trump, it was a very rare moment of American bipartisanship and was meant to serve as restraint on the president.

In a conversation with Bob Woodward about Trump's staunch support for the Saudi crown prince, Trump reportedly told the author "I saved his ass … I was able to get Congress to leave him alone. I was able to get them to stop" and added that Saudi Arabia spent billions of dollars on US military hardware.⁵³ Most of Trump's support for the Saudi ruling family publicly centered on military sales and how important they were for the US economy. In fact, the weapons sales were at the heart of the ethical debate surrounding US involvement in the war in Yemen. As much as the Trump White House attempted to emphasize the strategic aspect of weapons sales and US-Saudi relations in general, by this point the American general public and even many US officials themselves had started to question both the legality and strategic expedience of US patronage over the kingdom. Not only was the Saudi military not able to effectively leverage those advanced weapons systems—including the world's third largest fleet of F-15 fighters—to win the war themselves, the perpetual allegations of war crimes committed using American manufactured weapons platforms put significant pressure on the US government.

The leadership in the US Department of Defense centered their justification on the argument that United States, presence in Saudi Arabia's military command gave them influence over targeting and enabled the United States to ensure that the Saudis adhered to international humanitarian law. During his testimony before Congress on October 3, 2018, one day after Jamal Khashoggi's murder, US CENTCOM commander Gen. Joseph Votel stressed that the Saudi military was listening to US military advisers and were following many of the recommendation on improving targeting and countering the Houthi ballistic missile threat. Responding to a question from a US senator on what would happen if the United States were to cut off refueling and any other military assistance to the Saudis, Gen. Votel insisted that United States presence gave them "placement, access and influence with Saudi Arabia". He argued that it was in the interest of the United States, Saudi Arabia, and civilians in Yemen for the United States to stay engaged.⁵⁴ Likewise, in a letter sent to congressional leaders in March 2018, Secretary of Defense Mattis urged Congress to not impose restrictions on the "noncombatant"and to continue "limited US military support" provided to the Saudis who, according to Mattis were "engaging in operations in its legitimate exercise of self-defense".⁵⁵ Mattis insisted that restricting US military support "could increase civilian casualties, jeopardize cooperation with our partners on counterterrorism, and reduce our influence with the Saudis—all of which would further exacerbate the situation and humanitarian crisis".⁵⁶ Mattis also warned members of Congress that a US withdraw would "embolden Iran to increase its support to the Houthis, enabling further ballistic missile strikes on Saudi Arabia and threatening vital shipping lanes in the Red Sea, thereby raising the risk of a regional war".[57] The US military leadership's position that protection for civilians would be far worse if the US government were to cut of its military assistance to the Saudis contradicted its own analysis of mounting civilian deaths in Yemen caused by Saudi air strikes.

In an exchange between Gen. Votel and Senator Elizabeth Warren (D-MA) during a Senate Armed Services committee hearing in March 2018, the CENTCOM commander was asked: "General Votel, does CENTCOM track the purpose of the missions it is refueling? In other words, where a U.S.-refueled aircraft is going, what targets it strikes, and the result of the mission?"[58] Not only did Votel deny foreknowledge of Saudi targets, he also reported that CENTCOM was unable to tell if "U.S. fuel or U.S. munitions" were used after a Saudi air strike had occurred.[59] Votel's denial again contradicted his own argument that US presence and assistance would deter Saudi pilots from targeting civilians. In interviews with the *New York Times*, ten current and former US officials portrayed a fractious US response to ongoing reports of Yemeni civilians killed in coalition air strikes. Notwithstanding public denials, former senior State Department official said that the United States had access to records of every air strike over Yemen since the early days of the war, including the warplane and munitions used.[60] This was eventually confirmed during a 2019 Senate testimony in which Gen. Votel confirmed that CENTCOM did in fact have "access to a database detailed every air strike, warplane, target, munitions used and a brief description of the attack".[61] Tom Malinowski, a former Assistant Secretary of State, stated:

> In the end, we concluded that they were just not willing to listen ... They were given specific coordinates of targets that should not be struck and they continued to strike them. That struck me as a willful disregard of advice they were getting.[62]

The US government exerted no influence over Saudi Arabia. While the US military and the White House maintained that the United States needed to help Saudi Arabia defend itself against the Iranian government and its proxy in Yemen, the Saudi military carried out its military campaign without regard for US interests.

By the end of the Trump administration, there was growing frustration within the Department of State that Yemen had devolved into a self-created humanitarian crisis with no end in sight. US diplomats were well aware that US-supplied military equipment and support for the Saudis had caused and perpetuated the conflict and ultimately the humanitarian crisis.[63] Not only did the US Department of State face increasing pressure from Congress over alleged war crimes of allied forces assisted by United States refueling missions and the deteriorating humanitarian situation in Yemen, it paradoxically caused the Office of Weapons Removal and Abatement to provide more than $18.5 million between 2016 and 2019 to clear the very same unexploded ordnances the United States had given to the Saudis.[64] According to a *Washington Post* analysis, the US government played a significant part in the coalition's campaign and provided either arms, training, or maintenance support to the majority of the fighter jet squadrons during the conflict. This analysis also found that as many as 94 US contracts were awarded to individual Saudi and UAE squadrons since the onset of the war in 2015.[65] The analysis concluded that:

> a review of more than 900 publicly available sales announcements revealed that the four squadrons from Saudi Arabia that fly F-15S/SA planes benefited—and the remaining 15 squadrons probably benefited—from U.S. weapons and equipment contracts signed after the start of the war.[66]

It also found that the "US participated in joint exercises with at least 80% of squadrons that flew airstrike missions in Yemen. At least four times, these exercises took place on U.S. soil".[67] As early as 2016, observers at the UN Security Council and Human Rights Council stated that the United States "runs interference for the coalition, facilitating a culture of impunity in Yemen and diminishing pressure to achieve an immediate ceasefire".

From the onset of the war, Yemenis widely associated the United States with the war crimes committed by the Gulf coalition during the campaign.[68] Both officials in the Department of State and members of Congress bemoaned the humanitarian crisis that the war had caused. The numerous testimonies before Congress by CENTCOM reflect the extent to which US politicians seemed sensitive to media scrutiny and perceptions that the US government was at least partly responsible for alleged coalition war crimes. Yet despite continuous political pressure on the US government by human rights organizations, the US government appeared to rely on its own interpretation of US laws concerning military assistance to foreign armed forces. The "Leahy Laws" prohibits the US government from providing security assistance to foreign armed forces that "are credibly implicated in the commission of a gross violation of human rights". White House legal counsel has interpreted these laws to require the "vetting of units … when the security assistance—be it training, equipment or other assistance—is financed by the State Department or Defense Department ...".[69] Through a loophole that appears contrary to the spirit of the Leahy Laws, because Saudi Arabia and the UAE pay for all of their assistance through foreign military sales or direct commercial sales, these restrictions do not seem to apply.[70]

According to a 2022 GAO report, the US Air Force has conducted quarterly seminars for military officer in Saudi Arabia since 2018. These seminars focused on civilian harm mitigation and covered topics as targeting, civilian casualty investigations, and the law of armed conflict.[71] In addition to the Department of Defense's advisory role, the Department of State too provided civilian harm mitigation advice at various times between 2015 and 2017 and helped establish the Joint Incidents Assessment Team as an oversight body for the coalition's actions in Yemen.[72] Notwithstanding these efforts to safeguard international humanitarian law, US officials admitted to the GAO in 2022 that neither the Department of Defense nor the Department of State had determined "the extent to which US military support provided to Saudi Arabia and UAE has contributed to or reduced civilian harm in Yemen". More significantly, despite indications that US-origin defense articles seemed to have been used in what would constitute war crimes, neither US agency has conducted any investigations of any incidents of potential unauthorized use of US-origin equipment during the war.[73]

Nowhere in Yemen was the US government's contradictory role more evident than in the battle over Hodeidah where the belligerents fought for control over humanitarian aid supplies and food production. In September 2018, the UN lost access to Hodeidah's Red Sea Mills, the country's most important food storage facility holding 51,000 tons of grain, which was enough to feed more than 3.7 million people for a month.[74] At the time 14 million Yemenis were on severely malnourished. Houthis had controlled the mill for six months and when the World Food Program took over again in February 2019, most of the grain supplies had rotted.[75] The mills had also been booby-trapped with IED's by Houthis forces. It took the US Department of State's local partner, the Yemeni Mine Action Center, four months in 2019 to clear the mills. Funded by the US government, the Yemeni Mine Action Center also had to demine the port of Hodeidah in order for humanitarian assistance deliveries to resume; the entire port had been mined by Houthi forces prior to their departure, but also was full of unexploded, American-manufactured cluster munition from Saudi kinetic strikes.[76] The Red Sea Mills epitomized the paradoxical quagmire the United States had created through its blind eye to the Saudi indiscriminate use of force: the United States was funding the removal of weapons that it had provided to the Saudis.

During his presidential campaign, Joe Biden vowed that the Saudis would "pay the price, and make them in fact the pariah that they are". He went so far as to say that there was "very little social redeeming value in the present government in Saudi Arabia".[77] However, once Biden was in the White House, those promises would not fully translate into new foreign policy toward the kingdom. Although Biden did declassify and release the US intelligence report that had concluded that the Crown Prince Mohammed bin Salman himself had ordered the assassination, the Biden administration declined to impose any sanctions against him. Rather, the US Department of the Treasury's Office of Foreign Assets Control (OFAC) designated Ahmad Hassan Mohammed al Asiri, Saudi Arabia's former Deputy Head of General Intelligence Presidency and Saudi Arabia's Rapid Intervention Force the responsible parties for the murder of journalist Jamal Khashoggi and froze their assets in the United States.[78] Essentially, Biden released the evidence that implicated Salman for the murder but did not punish him for it. In many ways, it was more of a virtue signal to Democrats in Congress than an actual punitive measure against the Saudi leadership. It mirrored Biden's position on the Houthis: he revoked the Trump administration's designation of Houthis as "foreign terrorist organization" in order to guarantee access for humanitarian aid inside the country, but maintained the terrorist designation of Houthi leaders:

> Ansarallah leaders Abdul Malik al-Houthi, Abd al-Khaliq Badr al-Din al-Houthi, and Abdullah Yahya al-Hakim remain sanctioned under E.O. 13611 related to acts that threaten the peace, security, or stability of Yemen. We will continue to closely monitor the activities of Ansarallah and its leaders and are actively identifying additional targets for designation, especially those responsible for explosive boat attacks against commercial shipping in the Red Sea and UAV and missile attacks into Saudi Arabia. The United States will also continue to support the implementation of UN sanctions imposed on members of Ansarallah and will continue to call attention to the group's destabilizing activity and pressure the group to change its behavior.

> The United States remains clear-eyed about Ansarallah's malign actions, and aggression, including taking control of large areas of Yemen by force, attacking U.S. partners in the Gulf, kidnapping

and torturing citizens of the United States and many of our allies, diverting humanitarian aid, brutally repressing Yemenis in areas they control, and the deadly attack on December 30, 2020 in Aden against the cabinet of the legitimate government of Yemen. Ansarallah's actions and intransigence prolong this conflict and exact serious humanitarian costs.[79]

More importantly, in a far-reaching foreign policy speech in February 2021, Biden demanded for the war in Yemen to end and declared that his government was "ending all American support for offensive operations in the war in Yemen, including relevant arms sales".[80] By the time the President had updated Congress about remaining US deployments overseas in December 2022, as required by the War Powers Resolution, Biden disclosed that a small number of military personnel remained deployed inside Yemen "to conduct operations against al-Qa'ida in the Arabian Peninsula and ISIS".[81] Biden emphasized that remaining US military forces in Saudi Arabia were helping to "protect United States forces and interests in the region against hostile action by Iran and Iran-backed groups". By the end of Biden's first year, a total of 2,120 US troops remained in the kingdom and continued to "provide air and missile defense capabilities and support the operation of United States fighter aircraft".[82] The President repeated his emphasis that the US role in Saudi Arabia was purely defensive in nature:

> As reported previously, I directed an end to the United States support for the Saudi-led Coalition's offensive military operations against the Houthis in Yemen. United States Armed Forces, in a non-combat role, continue to provide military advice and limited information to regional forces for defensive and training purposes only as they relate to the Saudi-led Coalition's campaign against the Houthis in Yemen. Such support does not involve United States Armed Forces in hostilities with the Houthis for the purposes of the War Powers Resolution.[83]

While the Biden administration insisting that the US government had ceased "offensive" support for the Saudis, the reality of that ostensible policy change remained ambiguous. It appeared that the United States was still acting as super patron against Iran by means of using Saudi Arabia as proxy. Asked by members of Congress in April 2021 on how the US government was implementing the end of supporting offensive operations in Yemen, the Biden administration's envoy to Yemen, Tim Lenderking, said he did not know the remaining extent of US military involvement. Rather, Lenderking replied "I do think that we need to make sure that Saudi Arabia is able to defend itself ... but my focus is driving toward a ceasefire, so we can get out of this whole question of offensive and defensive weapons".[84]

The Biden administration also moved ahead with the weapons sales to the UAE worth $23.37 billion, including 50 F-35 warplanes and up to 18 MQ-9B armed drones as well as a package of air-to-air and air-to-ground munitions. The decision was widely denounced by human rights organizations in the US.[85] Department of State officials communicated to the GAO in their audit of US weapons sales that they made efforts to distinguish between offensive and defensive operations in FMS transfer decisions. In an effort to highlight the policy change under Biden, State Department officials noted an FMS transfer in November 2021 to Saudi Arabia for advanced medium range air-to-air missiles, which State emphasized could only be used to defend against cross-border aerial attacks and could not be used to engage ground targets.[86] Most fundamentally, the US government's support for Saudi defense reflected its continuation of military operations inside Yemen. As a report by the Brookings Institute noted: "the president stated that he would 'end U.S. support for offensive operations in Yemen'. Yet the Saudi-led war on Yemen by definition, is an offensive operation. Saudi Arabia is bombing and blockading another country".[87] Moreover, the transition from the Trump administration to the Biden administration did little to meaningfully alter Saudi tactics in Yemen despite the narrative put forth by the incoming administration (Figure 5.3). Looking at coalition air strikes during the Trump presidency, ACLED reports 11,052 coalition-launched air strikes, averaging to about 7.6 air strikes per day across Trump's time in office. The average number of SLC air strikes did somewhat decrease since Biden has taken office—3,348 air strikes through May 2022 resulting in an average of 6.9 daily strikes. Although this decrease is statistically significant ($p < 0.01$), it does not translate into a meaningful improvement for the Yemeni people. Throughout the Trump administration's laissez-faîre approach to Saudi Arabia, there was an average of 10.7 daily fatalities from coalition strikes; since Biden took office and despite his harsh rhetoric, there has been no statistically meaningful change in daily fatalities, which average just over ten deaths from coalition air strikes per day ($p = 0.20$). Additionally, the Biden administration continued American military support for Riyadh including the refueling of Saudi fighter jets, and has shown no attempt to call for an end to the Saudi coalition's blockade of all of Yemen's ports. As mentioned earlier, by late of 2021, the Biden State

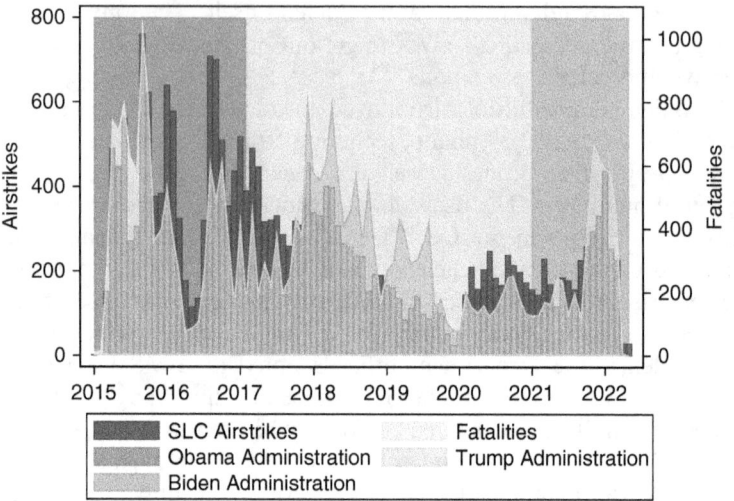

Figure 5.3 SLC Air Strikes and Lethality over US Administrations.

Department would approve weapons sales worth $1.15 billion; in contrast, the much criticized, last-minute sales approved by a lame-duck Trump administration were worth only about half that ($640 million) with the most recent previous authorized sale, albeit hefty at $2.7 billion, being in May 2019.[88]

By and large, none of the three US administrations exerted any meaningful control over Saudi Arabia. Despite US defense officials continued insistence that a US military presence was needed to guide Saudi Air Force attacks and to help reinforce territorial defenses and the Saudi's clear reliance on US weapons platforms, the Saudi government and its coalition partners continuously ignored pleas from embedded US military advisers for more caution. They recognized that the combination of coalition air strikes coupled with the blockade was feeding into a catastrophic humanitarian disaster without any real progress toward the coalition's goals. None of the American administrations, despite their differing rhetoric and distinct approaches to Saudi Arabia, displayed any real influence over their proxies nor the resolve to enforce demanded restraints on coalition targeting of civilians. Absent progress along the battlefront, the lack of effective Saudi statecraft only decreased the already lacking legitimacy of the Hadi government, which in essence served at the pleasure of the coalition. The Saudis too held little legitimacy amongst the Yemeni people. Their attention to citizen wellbeing throughout the war was nonexistent, they showed little interest in Yemen as anything other than a security and economic instrument, and despite their seemingly never-ending arsenal of expensive, high-tech weapons, they displayed no ability to coherently transform their on-paper military advantage into command of the battlefield or effective political engineering to aid in governing the country. In a way, the Saudis seemed stuck. They were neither capable of winning the war nor willing to abate the humanitarian disaster it had caused.

The 2019 evoking of the War Powers Act in response to American underwriting of the Saudi's campaign in Yemen was an initial public censure of the US government's support for the war, but it also represented an official statement of congressional disapproval for Saudi leadership itself. Biden had campaigned on isolating Saudi Arabia and announced that his incoming administration would end US support for Saudi offensive military operations. Biden's rhetoric was a signal to the Saudis that the war must end despite the ambiguity of how this demand would translate into US policy. Because Biden had openly chastised the Saudi crown prince for the Khashoggi murder and promised a toughening of US-Saudi relations as a means of distinguishing his foreign policy orientation from that of his predecessor, Biden had locked himself toward these ends or else face audience costs that could affect him and his party negatively in future elections.[89] He intended to use this tougher US position to ultimately force Saudi rulers into making peace.

Domestically, the US government's use of Saudi Arabia as a proxy to offshore balance against Iran initially seemed to carry few political risks. The strategic relationship between Saudi Arabia and the United States had enjoyed strong bipartisan support for over half a century. It seemed impervious to political shock and scandal. Following the 9/11 terrorist attacks, in which 15 of 19 hijackers were Saudi nationals, the Bush administration repeatedly reaffirmed the United States' close relationship with Saudi Arabia. In 2016, President Obama attempted to shield Saudi Arabia against a recently passed law that would allow the families of 9/11 victims to sue the Saudi government for wrongful death through his veto power; although congress rebuked Obama and by extension the Saudis with an exceptionally rare veto-override, the president's control over the declassification and release of documents related to alleged Saudi knowledge or involvement in the 9/11 attacks limits the impact of this law.[90]

This created peculiar foreign policy culture in Washington in which US attitudes toward Iran were framed along idealist lines while policy toward Saudi Arabia along realist ones. Human rights abuses in Iran were decried by the US government, whereas Saudi Arabia's authoritarian rule was seen with pragmatism because of the purported strategic value of bilateral relations. The alliance with Riyadh has centered around the assumption that even though the kingdom may be an authoritarian regime with a poor human rights record, strong military-to-military relations with would ultimately bear political and security dividends for the United States and the wider region.[91] This foreign policy paradox was particularly event during Trump's first state visit to Saudi Arabia in 2017. Praising the country for its counter-terrorism operations, even though the regime is a sponsor and promoter of radical Wahhabism and thousands of Saudi citizens had joined ISIS since its emergence, during a press conference in Riyadh that was reserved only for foreign press, Secretary of State Rex Tillerson denounced Iran's human rights standard while ignoring Saudi Arabia's.[92] With only rare exceptions such as the 9/11 Victims Act referenced above, the political contract between the United States and Saudi Arabia largely allowed Riyadh to act as an American proxy free from scrutiny by Congress. According to a senior congressional staffer, Saudi misconduct is not a priority for members of Congress because it is not something that voters care about. Even if members are cognizant of geopolitics and Middle East security, no member of Congress stands to gain anything from putting pressure on the administration over the US's role in Yemen. While this is partly due to American voters who are notoriously uninterested, under-informed, or ill-informed in matters of foreign policy,[93] it also reflects Congress's ceding of its constitutional role in foreign policy to the executive branch.[94] Moreover, much like domestic bills, foreign policy legislation is being fast-tracked by lobbyists and leadership rather than committees causing congressional knowledge about foreign affairs to fade away. This is particularly the case for weapon sales overseas.[95] Between 2015 and 2021, the Department of Defense administered at least $54.6 billion of military support to Saudi Arabia and the United Arab Emirates.[96] Missiles, including air-launched, ground-launched and sea-launched represented the greatest value (34%) of defense articles to both countries. A total of $18.8 billion in missiles alone was sold to Saudi Arabia and the UAE during that time. In addition to those missile sales, the United States authorized the sales of:

- $17.3 billion in military hardware, including ships, aircraft, weapons platforms, ammunition, radar, and communications systems (32%);
- $4.9 billion for special activities (9%);
- $2.8 billion for training (5%);
- $10.8 billion in equipment maintenance, construction, and other services (20%).[97]

Much of the training provided by the US Department of Defense to both Saudi and Emirati armed forces was intended to reduce civilian harm during military missions, including training at the Saudi War College that focused on the law of armed conflict including laws related to air-to-ground targeting in 2017, 2018, 2019, and 2020. Under a Foreign Military Sales (FMS) case agreed by President Trump in 2017, Saudi Arabia also received training on targeting capabilities, which DOD officials noted aimed to reduce civilian harm. The program included technical assistance for digital precision strike software and collateral damage estimation.[98] This training is currently also provided to the UAE, which also has an active FMS case for training on targeting capabilities. In 2022, DOD security cooperation officials in UAE informed the Government Accountability Office that the training includes multiple courses that aim to reduce the incidence of civilian harm.[99] However, seven years into the conflict, neither agency has "fully determined the extent to which U.S. military support has contributed to civilian harm in Yemen". As a 2022 GAO report concluded:

> State officials said they consider civilian harm and use of equipment when considering potential Foreign Military Sales for Saudi Arabia and UAE. In addition, DOD and State officials said they have made some efforts to understand the extent to which U.S.-origin defense articles were used in Yemen. However, despite several reports that airstrikes and other attacks by Saudi Arabia and UAE have caused extensive civilian harm in Yemen, DOD has not reported and State could not provide evidence that it investigated any incidents of potential unauthorized use of equipment transferred to Saudi Arabia or UAE.[100]

Both DoD and State had effectively created and maintained a framework of inaction with regards to making weapons sales contingent on adhering to the laws of war, reflecting an apparent decision to prioritize its strategic interests as a super patron over its moral obligation to minimize civilian suffering. Despite the training provided to both UAE and Saudi militaries, the United States would decline to make sales conditional on respect humanitarian law and the avoidance of war crimes. American political will, it seems, was lacking; accountability remains elusive.

Iran

From the onset of the Houthi takeover, the Iranian government's intention in Yemen was to keep the Houthi-run government in power in an effort to balance against Saudi Arabia by propping up an adversary along its border. When the Iranian government entered the conflict as a patron for the Houthis, it was the only external actor to have both extensive experience with irregular and proxy warfare and to be largely considered a legitimate external patron by their proxy. One Yemeni politician noted that while Iran did not want an endless war when it entered the conflict on the side of the Houthis, the prolonged fight certainly benefited Iran as it was not only drowning Saudi resources, but also showing Saudi vulnerability to ballistic missile and drone attacks from inside Yemen.[101] Moreover, politicians in Yemen were aware of the fact that Iran wanted a strong and independent Yemen, but that the Iranian government was also conscious of there being no control over the country without Houthis.[102] By 2022, Houthis continued to dominate the military balance in the country, were able to hold and control territory and, most importantly, remained capable of firing ballistic missiles into Saudi territory with the assistance of Iran's political and military support. Unlike the relationship between the Saudi and Yemeni governments, Houthi relations with Iran seemed far more equal; Houthis were Iranian partners, while the Yemeni government was subordinate to Saudi Arabia and UAE. Lacking Saudi Arabia's history of interference in Yemen and with Houthis being Zaydi Shi'as, Iran not only shared an ideological imprint with their proxy but also enjoyed far more legitimacy than Saudis and their coalition partners. At the same time, a Yemeni politician observed that while Houthis support Iran, "it is non unconditional as they not only see themselves differently from Shi'as, [Zaydi] doctrine also continued to hold off the Iranians from exerting too much control throughout the period".[103] On balance, Iranian efforts proved superior to Saudi Arabia not only because Iranian commandos were assisting their proxies with tactical support in battle, but also because Houthi leadership was given more autonomy from Tehran compared to the Yemeni government's relationship to Riyadh. Both policy and rhetoric from the Iranian government framed the relationship as one not between patron and proxy but between two allies. Whereas Saudis determined day-to-day management even at the local level for the Yemeni government, Houthis enjoyed more autonomy but also largely perceived Iran as legitimate partner.[104] The Iranian government was not only set on helping Houthis control Yemen, but also elevated them as the legitimate government internationally. To that end, the Iranian government officially handed custody of the Yemeni Embassy in Tehran over to Houthi officials on November 19, 2019. In an effort to signal its allegiance to Iran, Houthi representatives met with both

Hamas and Iranian officials, and a spokesman for Houthi forces spokesman attested to the Houthi military's readiness to respond to potential Israeli threats.[105] In 2020, Iran appointed Hassan Eirlo as ambassador to Yemen. Eirlo was a commander within the IRGC Quds Force, had previously served in the Iran-Iraq War, and helped train Hezbollah fighters to operate anti-aircraft equipment in the 1990s. At the time, the appointment of a high profile IRGC commander as ambassador just when the UN weapons embargo against Iran was lifted indicated Iranian commitment to increase not only arms shipments to Houthis but also further cement political relations with Houthis and "solidify their position" within what the US military called Iran's regional Threat Network.[106]

Iranian support for Houthis had commenced prior to the war. In 2013, two years before the Houthi takeover, US and Yemeni forces confiscated Chinese QW-1M anti-aircraft missiles from a vessel off the coast. When Houthis took over the government in 2015, they acquired a substantial arsenal of weapons after seizing the government stockpile of mostly Soviet-era short-range ballistic missiles (SRBMs) and Surface-to Air Missiles (SAMs).[107] This stockpile would have depleted had it not been for Iranian resupply of sophisticated military weaponry. In October 2016, Houthi forces fired anti-ship rockets at an UAE military vessel in the Bab el Mandeb Strait, destroying it. To US military intelligence, the use of this particular new powerful anti-ship rocket indicated an apparent change in both Houthi tactics and resources, enabling Houthis to target ships at some distance from the Yemeni shoreline. This new capability prompted the US Navy to declare the group as an active threat in the Red Sea Strait.[108] More significantly, it was a watershed moment when belligerents in Yemen and the US government noted the arrival of advanced weapons to Houthis, signaling a more material Iranian involvement in the conflict.

Ultimately, Iranian contributions to the Houthi arsenal brought significant impacts to the military balance. It not only helped Houthis fight the Yemeni government, but it also expanded Houthi's abilities to strike Saudi Arabia and coalition members through their expanded ballistic missiles and UAV capabilities, and dramatically increased the precision of Houthi attacks. For example, while early long-range strikes into Saudi territory lacked precision, once Houthis acquired land-attack cruise missiles and had access to better intelligence collection, the accuracy of missile attacks improved significantly.[109] As far as attacks against ground forces inside Yemen and air defenses against coalition air strikes were concerned, field research inside the country suggested that "Houthis were able to use anti-tank-guided missiles (ATGMs) perhaps most effectively of all weapons, which along with the use of surface-to-air missiles (SAMs) increases casualties and equipment loss".[110] Iran maintained a sophisticated smuggling infrastructure that supplied Houthis forces with anti-tank, anti-ship, landattack-cruise, and surface-to-air missile components. Various maritime interdictions by coalition forces and Yemen's coast guard during the war showed that Iranian assistance provided the Houthis with anti-aircraft weapon systems such as LACMs, ATGMs, and components for UAVs. A report prepared for the US military in December 2020 concluded that:

> Houthis have shown that the effectiveness of these weapons, even when lethality is relatively low, can be maximized when combined with intelligence and precision against high- value targets (HVTs) to demoralize forces and rattle global energy markets, which poses significant force protection challenges.[111]

The Iranians amplified their proxy's capabilities enough that Houthis were able to fight both their domestic adversary as well their opponent's external patrons. Iran supplied Houthis will high-end weaponry through smuggling routes in Houthi-controlled territory, ranging from Tomahawk-sized autonomous missiles, guided and unguided missiles to small arms. When the UN-arms embargo against Iran was lifted in October 2020 (having been in place since 2007), weapons inflows to Houthis also increased substantially. Iran's Quds Force provided extensive tactical support on the ground and, according to US military in Yemen, acted as a force multiplier to Houthis forces.[112] In addition to expanded missile capabilities, Houthis were able to plant hundreds of sea mines and water-born improvised explosive devices in the Red Sea and Arabian Sea, directly threatening commercial traffic out of the Gulf. By 2020, it appeared that Houthis had started their own manufacturing of naval mines. In December 2020 alone, three naval mines collided with merchant ships in the Red Sea despite the Saudi coalition's mine removal efforts during that period. By interrupting naval traffic, Houthis not only showed the Saudi Coalition's vulnerabilities but also lessened international confidence in the safety of Red Sea shipping lanes, a key access point for Saudi and GCC's economic output.[113]

As mentioned, since the start of the conflict until 2022, Houthi forces' long-range weapon capability evolved considerably.[114] Specifically, having seizing Yemeni missile stocks in January 2015, Houthi forces would next acquire drone capabilities in December 2015. By October of the next year, they had successfully damaged a UAE naval vessel. A year later in October 2017, Houthi forces would intercept an incoming MQ-9 Reaper UAV for the first time. An attack targeting Riyadh was intercepted by Saudi aid defense in November 2017. This attack demonstrated the Houthis expanded range and that the Saudi capital was now directly threatened. Over the next several years, Houthis would successfully execute precision strikes against high-ranking military targets in Yemen while also threatening coalition countries' infrastructure; they would successfully strike Saudi Arabia's East-West oil pipeline in May 2017, the Jeddah Aramco facilities in November 2020 and March 2022, and the Ras Tanura and Rabigh refineries in March 2022; in January 2022, two Houthi-fired ballistic missiles would be intercepted near Abu Dhabi, UAE.[115]

These effects are apparent when looking at targeting patterns of Houthi remote violence, which are presented in Figure 5.4. The ACLED project identifies 9,972 regional missile or artillery attacks originating from Houthi forces, which are divided between targets internal to Yemen and those in neighboring coalition countries or offshore. The apparent decrease of missile usage in early 2016 reflects the exhaustion of the initial arsenal Houthi forces seized in 2015. By late 2016, Houthi forces recommence widespread missile attacks, with a significant portion of those attacks striking targets external to Yemen over the next two years. It was not until 2018 that Houthis had any meaningful drone

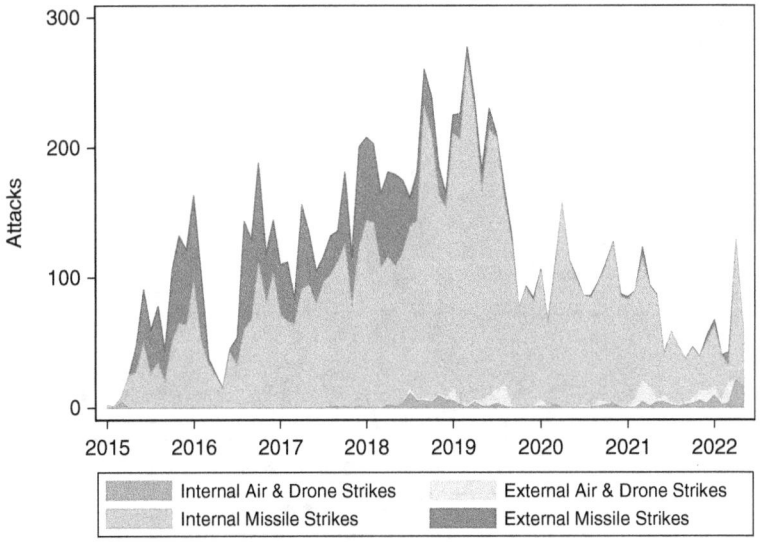

Figure 5.4 Targeting of Houthi Missile Strikes.

capabilities, however once they gain drone capabilities, the relative use of missiles against external targets declines. Throughout the conflict, approximately 20% of Houthi missile strikes (1,949 of 9,972) have targets outside of Yemen. In contrast, once Houthis gain drone capabilities, nearly half (49%) of launched drone attacks have external targets (155 of 315).

Figure 5.4 also illustrates that cross-border UAV and missile attacks increased substantially after 2018, prompting the Saudis to increase their focus on aerial defense of the kingdom significantly. Houthi missile and UAV capability could now reach deep into Saudi territory, forcing the Saudis to increase their focus on defending their own territory from external attack. Figure 5.5 shows this uptick in ranged attacks against targets within Saudi Arabia, but also Saudi Arabia's efforts to intercept those attacks.[116] A majority of those air attacks initially targeted sites in Jizan and Asir provinces just across the Yemeni border. By 2019 missiles and UAV attacks had struck Aramco facilities and airports on both the Red Sea and the Persian Gulf coasts. In a dramatic display of long-range capability, on March 4, 2021 Houthis claimed to have used a Quds-2 cruise missile to target an Aramco facility in Jeddah, approximately 700 km up the Red Sea coast from Yemen. It was during this period that Houthis forces also conducted "Operation Balance of Deterrence", which included the

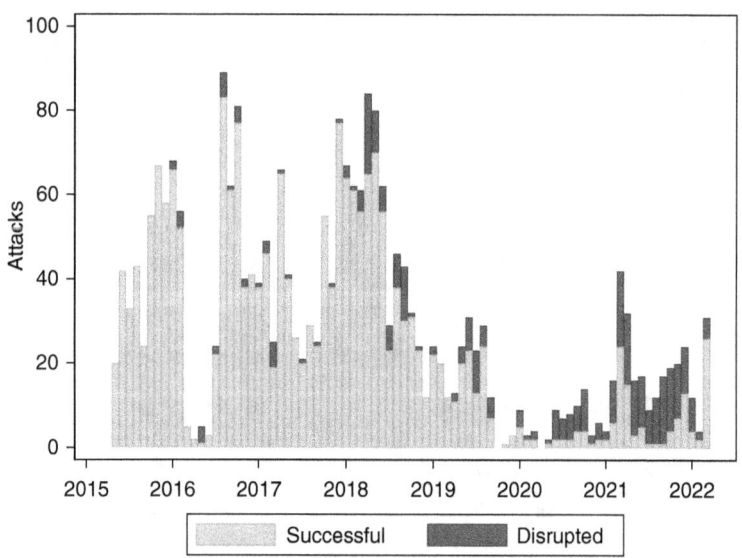

Figure 5.5 Houthi Ranged Attacks Targeting Saudi Arabia.

targeting of Aramco facilities in Dhahran and Ras Tanura port on the Persian Gulf, some 1,200 km from Houthi-controlled territory.[117] By late 2019 and early 2020, numerous maritime interdictions of UAVs and missile components indicated that Iran had stepped up its resupply methods to their proxy. Reports to the US military showed that cross-border smuggling operations increased, stating that

> this high tempo cross-border attacks indicate new smuggling routes or varied methods are being employed to resupply Houthi arsenals. Additionally, the regularity in which the Houthis appear capable of striking deep into Saudi territory became a growing concern as advanced, long-range weapon systems from Iran make their way into Yemen.[118]

While Iranian supply routes maintained Houthi force's stock of ballistic missiles, Iranian military hardware also proved vital in Houthi air defenses. The Houthis' major pivot to strengthening air defenses and repelling Saudi attacks seemed to have occurred in 2019. Using what appeared to be an Iranian-supplied Rapier Battery system, Houthis downed a Saudi F15 fighter, a coalition Apache helicopter, and a Saudi Wing Loong reconnaissance UAV in November 2019. Houthis also publicly showcased and used the Tahqeb-1 (a Russian-made R-73 air-to-air missile converted to SAM use) and Fater-1 (a Russian-made SA-6 surface-to-air missile) as air defense systems.[119] Then in the battle in Marib in 2021, Houthis used not only new surface-to-air missiles but also new air defense systems. On March 7, 2021, Houthi spokesman Brig. Gen. Yahya Saree' announced that their air defense systems shot down a Saudi UAV in al-Jawf governorate, close to the Marib border. The UAV was identified as a Turkish manufactured Karayel, and Saree' credited a new surface-to-air missile for the successful downing. Likewise on the same day, Saudi authorities released footage that purportedly showed a SLC aircraft destroying a Houthi air defense system they identified as an SA-6.[120] While Saudi air support to Yemeni forces proved a vital support role along front lines, Iranian supplied air-defense systems also checked Saudi air raids. By all account, Houthi military capabilities were dependent on Iranian supply lines and Houthi military operations benefted from Iranian tactical advice. Houthis would not have been able to continue the war without Iranian assistance.

Houthi dependency on Iran came at a political price though. Houthi governance within territories it controlled largely was a balancing act with tribal power. In fact, the entire security apparatus in Houthi-

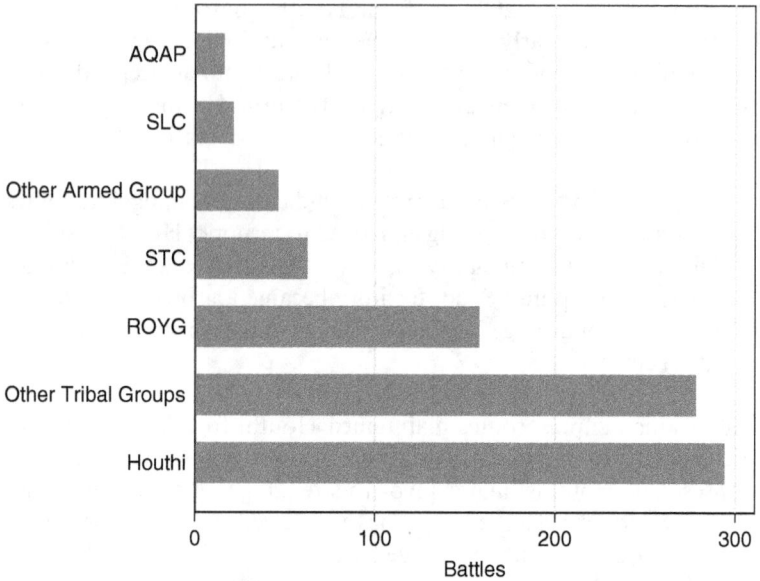

Figure 5.6 Tribal Participation in Battles.

controlled territory was depended on the respective Houthi leaders' ability to placate the local tribal population. Here a common Houthi practice was to aid tribes in settling disputes with rival tribes in exchange for loyalty. Tribes often clashed with one another, and in the context of the ongoing war, it was commonplace for tribal feuds to devolve into direct fighting between tribes. In fact, when tribal groups were a primary belligerent in a battle, the Houthis were the only group that tribes fought against more frequently than other tribes (Figure 5.6). Violent clashes between and Houthi forces throughout Houthi controlled territory showed that these types of agreements were "tenuous and dependent on compliance with tribal demands."[121] By and large, Houthis only governed at the mercy of the tribes. Tribes in their own right were an important factor in the national balance of power. According to observations by US military forces, tribes were instrumental in maintaining smuggling routes extending from the ports in Oman and along Yemen's extensive shoreline. As Yemen essentially only has one highway that spans the entire country, tribal control of routes was fundamental for Houthi access to Iranian weaponry. While illicit trafficking of goods had a long history in the country, US forces noted that the war "caused networks to switch form criminal to kinetic smuggling". Tribal elders, mainly in eastern governorates, dominated the East-West route of illicit weapon trafficking and oversaw a sophisticated network of checkpoints to protect the main routes. While tribal interests largely fell along economic lines rather than being politically motivated, their allegiance was subject to change to the highest bidder.[122]

An important inference here regarding the nature of the relationship between Houthis and tribes as well as between Houthis and their other domestic antagonists is that while the involvement of Iran and Saudi Arabia ultimately prolonged the civil war by propping up their respective surrogates to the detriment of Yemen's population, Yemeni actors never fought along sectarian lines. A politician close to the Muslim Brotherhood in Yemen observed that although Saudi Arabia and Iran may have exacerbated the sectarian aspect of the war, the inherent complexity of Yemeni society was the main reason that full-fledged sectarian conflict, like that in seen Syria or Iraq, never emerged. The war in Yemen, for Yemeni people at least, had always been over control over the state rather than sectarian or ideological lines. While this did not make the conflict less dangerous for the civilian population, belligerents largely treated prisoners and captives well and agreed to periodic prisoner exchanges. The politician noted that there was an element of "co-existence" even during the most intense phases of the war and that civilians living in territories under Houthi control remained largely unharmed by the Houthi security apparatus.[123] Notwithstanding the relative lack of sectarian violence, Houthis still weaponized humanitarian aid and, as observed by US military forces in the country, were trying to exploit civil vulnerabilities. The distribution of aid, coupled with concerted Houthi propaganda was used to win over subjugated civilian populations.[124]

Conclusion

The intervention by external patrons both protracted the civil war and made it far more destructive for the civilian population. Supply lines from the United States to Saudi Arabia and from Iran to Houthis contributed to an ongoing military stalemate in which neither belligerent was able to decisively win the conflict. While Houthis largely emerged as the dominant force with regards to both territorial control and its offensive posture toward Saudi Arabia, a political settlement remained elusive. While the Trump administration maintained a largely unconditional position toward Saudi Arabia's military operations despite the Saudi leadership's alleged crimes, it did carry some domestic political costs. Likewise, the Biden administration's sharp did not necessarily change the nature of US support for Saudi Arabia, nor did it take meaningful efforts to curb Saudi propensity to "inadvertently" catch civilians in the crossfire. Rather, President Biden's "farewell" to underwriting "offensive operations" by Saudis against Yemen appeared to be a veneer, largely maintaining the same policy general policy he inherited from his predecessor and had himself helped shape during the Obama administration. We uncover no evidence that would indicate the United States possessed any real influence over the Saudi government, though there was also little evidence of effort to influence the Saudis that would go beyond virtue signaling for domestic audiences. Despite its steady access to advanced weaponry and even when it was clearly misusing that weaponry, the Saudi leadership could not transform its on-paper military dominance to achieve victory or politically engineer a mutually acceptable solution. Both, the United States as the super patron and Saudi Arabia as the patron over the Yemeni government possessed power, but respectively lacked influence.

Iran, for its part enjoyed more legitimacy in the eyes of their surrogate. They provided tactical support on the battlefield while also granting Houthis the autonomy to conduct the war themselves. However, Houthi dependency on procuring weapons from Iran while sharing ideological imprints with the Islamic Republic did not come without political costs at home. Notwithstanding concerted propaganda efforts in Houthi-controlled territory, polls conducted indicate that there are significant grievances against Houthi governance.[125] Polling across Houthi-controlled territory in late 2020 suggested that "Houthi religious doctrine, recruitment tactics, corruption, and other forms of poor governance have generated acute discontent among some demographics, particularly among young, educated individuals".[126] However, the polling conducted in the governorates of Amran, al-Bayda, Dhamar, Hajjah, al-Hodeidah, Ibb, Sana'a, and Sadaa, as well as Sana'a municipality revealed that the Houthis and the General People's Congress (GPC) were the most favored of all domestic and international actors. The GPC won the most favorable views (54%) of any actor, followed by Houthis which were viewed positively by 48%. Respondents indicated very negative perceptions of the United Arab Emirates (95%), STC (95%), United States (86%), and Saudi Arabia (84%).[127] Positive perceptions of Houthis largely fell along sectarian lines; of those who identified as Zaydi, 72% held favorable views of the Houthis as opposed to only 24% of those who identified as non- Zaydi.[128] Among military-aged Zaydis, there was reticence to fully embrace the Houthi movement, as many did not view the Houthis as representative of Zaidism. Likewise, educated Zaydis in the greater Sana'a metropolitan viewed Iran much less favorably than the Zaydi population overall.[129] By and large, a majority of constituents who remained in Houthi-controlled territory had positive or neutral views of Iran and negative perceptions of the Saudi-led coalition and Hadi government. Were they to govern, Houthis would need to navigate a complex two-level game. They would need to balance domestic alliances with tribes, which had significant clout in Yemeni politics. They would also need to heavily rely on anti-Saudi and anti-Hadi propaganda, not only to shift attention away from their own failures in governance but also portray themselves as an ally and partner to Iran, rather than appear the surrogate that Hadi had become.

These mixed perceptions of the external patrons also apply to in government-controlled territories. A poll conducted in Socotra Governorate in spring 2020 regarded the United Arab Emirates as the most favorable international actor, while Saudi Arabia received the least support from respondents. A majority of respondents also expressed support for southern secession, which could partially explain divergent perceptions of the two as UAE was more amenable to succession than Saudi Arabia.[130] There were also clear divisions between supporters of the UAE and Southern Transitional Council (STC) and supporters of the Yemeni government and al-Islah Party. Pollsters at the time regarded the archipelago as a representative microcosm of the South as attitudes there largely mirrored political divisions found elsewhere in the South. A total of 94% of respondents viewed the UAE favorably with 76% naming it the most trusted international actor. By contrast, 88% viewed the Saudi Arabia favorably, but fewer than 7% saw it as the most trusted actor.[131] Iran was seen as the least favorable external actor with 95% of respondents saying that it had the most negative impression on Yemen.[132]

In Houthi-controlled Amran governorate, the inverse was found in respondents' preferences, according to a poll conducted on fall 2019. While Iran and Hezbollah received the most favorable views (45% and 44%, respectively), Saudi Arabia was viewed favorably by only 34%, while the UAE was viewed unfavorably by 92% of respondents.[133] With coalition air strikes being regarded as the most dangerous threat to livelihoods, 73% of respondents in Amran believed that the Saudi Arabia and coalition partners acted in self-interests, with 54% not believing that the coalition was truly vested in the war's outcome.[134] Likewise, 76% of people who found coalition air strikes to be inaccurate also trusted Iran to play a role in ending the war. In contrast, "49% of respondents who believe that Iran and the Houthis were closely linked were markedly more likely to have negative views of Iran". For Yemenis, attitudes toward external actors appear heavily influenced by their individual experiences with those actors, especially in regards to the victimization of civilians and destruction of infrastructure (which was almost entirely caused by coalition air strikes). A highly polarized media and robust propaganda campaigns also shaped perspectives as opposing narratives of the war from pro-Houthi websites and social media outlets and pro-Saudi sources emerged.

After seven years of war, prospects for a political settlement remain elusive. Yemen is more fragmented than ever before and while the internationally recognized government continues to reside in Riyadh, Houthis maintain control of the capital and much of the country.

Notes

1 Summer Said and Stephen Kalin, "Saudi Arabia Pushed Yemen's Elected President to Step Aside, Saudi and Yemeni Officials Say", *The Wall Street Journal* (17 April 2022), https://www.wsj.com/articles/saudi-arabia-pushed-yemens-elected-president-to-step-aside-saudi-and-yemeni-officials-say-11650224802 (accessed 22 April 2022).
2 Alexandra Stark, "The Monarch's Pawns? Gulf State Proxy Warfare 2011-Today", *New America* (15 June 2020), https://www.newamerica.org/international-security/reports/the-monarchs-pawns/ (accessed 1 June 2021).
3 Fearon 1994; Bueno de Mesquita et al. 2003; Weeks 2008.
4 See S.J.Res.7 - A joint resolution to direct the removal of United States Armed Forces from hostilities in the Republic of Yemen that have not been authorized by Congress (116th Congress, 2019–2020), https://www.congress.gov/bill/116th-congress/senate-joint-resolution/7/text (accessed 10 December 2020).
5 The US Defense Security Cooperation Agency documents approved foreign weapons sales on their website: https://www.dsca.mil/press-media/major-arms-sales (accessed 9 June 2022).
6 After the Biden administration vowed to end all US support for offensive operations in Yemen, it started to rely more on the UAE and resumed a proposed weapon deal worth $23.4 billion to the UAE. The deal which had been negotiated under the Trump administration includes F-35 fighter jets, armed drones, and associated missiles and bombs. Afrah Nasser, "US Resuming Arms Sales to UAE Is Disastrous" (15 April 2021), https://www.hrw.org/news/2021/04/15/us-resuming-arms-sales-uae-disastrous# (accessed 13 May 2021).
7 Interview with author.
8 Yahya al-Sewari, "Yemen's Al-Mahra: From Isolation to the Eye of a Geopolitical Storm", Sana'a Center for Strategic Studies (5 July 2019), https://sanaacenter.org/publications/analysis/7606 (accessed 28 April 2022).
9 Ibid.
10 Interview with author.

11 Interview with author.
12 Interview with author.
13 Declan Walsh and Eric Schmitt, "Arms Sales to Saudis Leave American Fingerprints on Yemen's Carnage", *The New York Times* (25 December 2018), https://www.nytimes.com/2018/12/25/world/middleeast/yemen-us-saudi-civilian-war.html (accessed 22 April 2022).
14 Ibid.
15 See Defense Security Cooperation Agency, Saudi Arabia- Blanket Order Training (5 June 2017), https://www.dsca.mil/press-media/major-arms-sales/saudi-arabia-blanket-order-training#:~:text=The%20estimated%20program%20cost%20is,Programs%20of%20Instruction%20(POIs) (accessed 22 April 2022).
16 Ibid.
17 Walsh and Schmitt 2018.
18 Ibid.
19 Ibid.
20 Bernd Kaussler. *Yemen Human Security Map*, James Madison University, https://sites.lib.jmu.edu/yemen-human-security-project/.
21 Interview with author.
22 Ibid.
23 Ibid.
24 Ibid.
25 Interview with author.
26 Ibid.
27 Department of State, Doc. FL-2018–06527 "Unclassified", https://foia.state.gov/Search/Results.aspx?searchText=(Yemen)%20AND%20(Yemen)&beginDate=20150101&endDate=20220622 (accessed 1 June 2022).
28 Interview with author.
29 Ibid.
30 Interview with author.
31 Open Statement of Yemen (11 November 2018), https://www.justsecurity.org/wp-content/uploads/2021/01/yemen-statement-former-obama-officials-november-11-2018.pdf (accessed 4 May 2022).
32 Missy Ryan, "Top Obama-Era Officials Urge Immediate End to U.S. Involvement in Yemen War", *The Washington Post* (11 November 2018), https://www.washingtonpost.com/world/national-security/top-obama-era-officials-urge-immediate-end-to-us-involvement-in-yemen-war/2018/11/10/ce8e8654-8d93-4dd2-9f68-822cb08b9f16_story.html (accessed 5 May 2022).
33 Ibid.
34 Human Rights Watch, "Obama Officials' Incomplete Reckoning with Failure on Yemen" (19 November 2018), https://www.hrw.org/news/2018/11/19/obama-officials-incomplete-reckoning-failure-yemen# (accessed 5 May 2022).
35 Committee on Homeland Security, US House of Representatives, Denying Safe Havens: Homeland Security's efforts to counter threats from Pakistan, Yemen, and Somalia (3 June 2011), https://www.govinfo.gov/content/pkg/CHRG-112hhrg72239/pdf/CHRG-112hhrg72239.pdf (accessed 22 May 2022).
36 Scott Shane, "The Lessons of Anwar al-Awlaki", *The New York Times* (27 August 2015), https://www.nytimes.com/2015/08/30/magazine/the-lessons-of-anwar-al-awlaki.html

37 The Bureau of Investigative Journalism, "Strikes in Yemen", https://www.thebureauinvestigates.com/projects/drone-war/charts?show_casualties=1&show_injuries=1&show_strikes=1&location=yemen&from=2008-1-1&to=2017-1-1 (accessed 20 May 2022).
38 The White House, Letter to the Speaker of the House and President Pro Tempore of the Senate Regarding the War Powers Report (7 December 2021), https://www.whitehouse.gov/briefing-room/statements-releases/2021/12/07/letter-to-the-speaker-of-the-house-and-president-pro-tempore-of-the-senate-regarding-the-war-powers-report-2/ (22 May 2022).
39 Nick Turse, "Will the Biden Administration Shine Light on Shadowy Special Ops Programs?", *The Intercept* (20 March 2021), https://theintercept.com/2021/03/20/joe-biden-special-operations-forces/ (21 May 2022).
40 Interview with author.
41 See tweet by Saudi Foreign Ministry (9 April 2019), https://mobile.twitter.com/ksamofaen/status/1115576359739363332 (accessed 12 May 2022).
42 Six months after leaving the White House, Kushner secured a $2 billion investment from a fund led by the Saudi crown prince, despite objections from the fund's advisers about the merits of the deal. David D. Kirkpatrick and Kate Kelly, "Before Giving Billions to Jared Kushner, Saudi Investment Fund Had Big Doubts", *The New York Times* (10 April 2022), https://www.nytimes.com/2022/04/10/us/jared-kushner-saudi-investment-fund.html (accessed 12 May 2022); Alan Rappeport, "Mnunchin's Private Equity Fund Raises $2.5 Billion", *The New York Times,* https://www.nytimes.com/2021/09/20/us/politics/mnuchin-saudi-private-equity.html (accessed 12 May 2022).
43 Helene Cooper, Thomas Gibbson-Neff, and Eric Schmitt, "Army Special Forces Secretly Help Saudis Combat Threat From Yemen Rebels", *The New York Times* (3 May 2018), https://www.nytimes.com/2018/05/03/us/politics/green-berets-saudi-yemen-border-houthi.html (accessed 20 May 2022).
44 Ibid.
45 Ibid.
46 In the tweet on June 6, 2017, Trump stated "During my recent trip to the Middle East I stated that there can no longer be funding of Radical Ideology. Leaders pointed to Qatar - look!" Patrick Wintour, "Donald Trump Tweets Support for Blockage Imposed on Qatar", *The Guardian* (6 June 2017), https://www.theguardian.com/world/2017/jun/06/qatar-panic-buying-as-shoppers-stockpile-food-due-to-saudi-blockade (accessed 13 May 2022).
47 In the testimony, Tillerson was asked by a committee aide about a dinner between Kushner and Steve Bannon with Saudi and UAE rulers in May 2017, in which the two leaders outlined their plan to impose an economic blockade on Qatar. Tillerson said he had no idea of the dinner before this. "It makes me angry", he said. "Because I didn't have a say. The State Department's views were never expressed". Robbie Gramer, "Tillerson to Kushner: We've Got to Stop Meeting Like This" (27 June 2019), https://foreignpolicy.com/2019/06/27/tillerson-secretary-of-state-testimony-transcript-house-foreign-affairs-committee-jared-kushner-role-trump-administration/ (accessed 12 May 2022).
48 Middle East Monitor, "Qatari Forces Deployed in Yemen Return Home", *Middle East Monitor* (8 June 2017), https://www.middleeastmonitor.com/

External Patrons of Surrogates 113

20170608-qatari-forces-deployed-in-yemen-return-home/ (accessed 21 May 2022).
49 Interview with author.
50 Because Qatar was completely cut off from the Saudi market and airspace, they had to redirect import and flight routes from Saudi Arabia via Iran. While for Qatar Airlines this added six hours to each flight, five years of blockade ultimately brought Doha closer to Tehran. Interview with author. By March 2022, the Iranian and Qatari governments had signed 14 agreements for greater cooperation in aviation, trade, shipping, media, cancellation of visa requirements, electricity, education, and culture. In a joint press conference in Doha, the Iranian president said, "We believe that the level of existing cooperation between the countries of the region is not commensurate with potential ties". He continued, "Iran seeks to enhance these relations as our goal is regional convergence". Anna. L. Jacobs, "Qatar and Iran Expand Ties Amid Broader Gulf De-escalation", The Arab Gulf States Institute in Washington (11 March 2022), https://agsiw.org/qatar-and-iran-expand-ties-amid-broader-gulf-de-escalation/ (accessed 13 May 2022).
51 Megan Keller, "Graham on Saudi Arabia: I Feel Completely Betrayed", *The Hill* (22 October 2022), https://thehill.com/homenews/senate/412558-graham-on-saudi-arabia-i-feel-completely-betrayed/ (accessed 12 May 2022).
52 S.J.Res.7 - To direct the removal of United States Armed Forces from hostilities in the Republic of Yemen that have not been authorized by Congress (116th Congress 2019–2020), https://www.congress.gov/bill/116th-congress/senate-joint-resolution/7/text (accessed 15 May 2022).
53 Bess Levin, "Report: Trump Bragged about Protecting Saudi Prince Whose Goons Dismembered a Journalist via Bone Saw", *Vanity Fair* (10 September 2020), https://www.vanityfair.com/news/2020/09/donald-trump-mbs-saved-his-ass (accessed 12 May 2022).
54 C-SPAN, "User Clip: General Votel Exchange with Senator Angus King concerning US Support to Saudi-Led Coalition" (3 October 2018), https://www.c-span.org/video/?c4753259/user-clip-general-votel-exchange-senator-angus-king-support-saudi-led-coalition (accessed 22 May 2022).
55 Karoun Demirjian, "Mattis Asks Congress Not to Restrict US Support for Saudi Bombing of Yemen" (14 March 2018), https://www.washingtonpost.com/powerpost/mattis-appeals-to-congress-not-to-pass-yemen-resolution-vote-expected-next-week/2018/03/14/b3c2c6b6–27d7–11e8–874b-d517e912f125_story.html (accessed 23 May 2022).
56 Ibid.
57 Ibid.
58 Zaid Jilani, "Military Breass Tells Congress It Has No Idea What Saudi Arabia Is Doing with US Bombs in Yemen", *The Intercept* (14 March 2018), https://theintercept.com/2018/03/14/yemen-war-centcom-elizabeth-warren/ (accessed 23 May 2022).
59 Ibid.
60 Declan Walsh and Eric Schmitt, "Arms Sales to Saudi Arabia Leave Fingerprints on Yemen's Carnage", *The New York Times* (25 December 2018), https://www.nytimes.com/2018/12/25/world/middleeast/yemen-us-saudi-civilian-war.html (accessed 23 May 2022).

61 Senator Elizabeth Warren, "Senator Warren Gets Answer from CENTCOM Commander about Yemen", https://www.youtube.com/watch?v=GjztJKUj0yA (accessed 1 July 2022).
62 Ibid.
63 Interview with author.
64 Between 2016 and 2019, the US Office for Weapons Removal and Abetment was engaged in following weapons destruction operations in Yemen:
   - Deployed 60 survey and clearance teams across Yemen responsible for clearing over 368,000 explosive hazards and over 23.6 million square meters, enabling the delivery of life saving humanitarian aid;
   - Created a training center in Aden and provided training to Yemeni deminers that equipped them with the skills needed to address complex explosive devices emplaced by Houthis;
   - Provided prosthetics and vocational training to more than 260 Yemeni men, women, and children allowing survivors of landmines and other explosives to maintain their independence and provide for themselves and their families;
   - Provided risk education to more than 1.2 million Yemeni men, women, and children, teaching them about potential dangers from explosive remnants of war (ERW) in their communities and encouraging safe behavior. US Department of State, Remarks and Releases-Bureau of Political-Military Affairs, US Conventional Weapons Destruction Program (2 April 2020), https://2017–2021.state.gov/u-s-conventional-weapons-destruction-program-yemen/index.html (accessed 23 May 2022); Interview with author.
65 Joyce Sohyun, Meg Kelly, and Atthar Mirza, "Saudi-Led Airstrikes in Yemen Have Been Called War Crimes. Many Relied on US Support", *The Washington Post* (4 June 2022), https://www.washingtonpost.com/investigations/interactive/2022/saudi-war-crimes-yemen/ (accessed June 2022).
66 Ibid.
67 Ibid.
68 US Department of State, Case No. F-2015–16997, Doc No. C06018219 (7 December 2016), https://foia.state.gov/Search/Results.aspx?searchText=(Yemen)%20AND%20(Yemen)&beginDate=20150101&endDate=20220622 (accessed 8 June 2022).
69 Sohyun et al. 2022.
70 Ibid.
71 US Government Accountability Office, "The Department of Defense (DOD) Administered at least $54.6 Billion of Military Support to Saudi Arabia and the United Arab Emirates (UAE) from Fiscal Years 2015 Through 2021" (June 2022), https://www.gao.gov/assets/gao-22-105988.pdf (accessed 1 August 2022).
72 Ibid.
73 Ibid.
74 MEE, "UN Resumes Grain Milling in Yemen's Hodeidah after Shelling-Induced Halt", *Middle East Eye* (6 January 2020), https://www.middleeasteye.net/news/un-resumes-grain-milling-after-brief-halt-yemen (accessed 23 May 2020).

75 Mina Aldroubi and Ali Mahmood, "UN Accesses Red Sea Mills amid Fears of Grain Rot", *The National* (27 February 2019), https://www.thenationalnews.com/world/mena/un-accesses-red-sea-mills-amid-fears-of-grain-rot-1.830997 (accessed 24 May 2022).
76 Interview with author.
77 David E. Sanger, "Candidate Biden Called Saudi Arabia a Pariah. He Now Has to Deal with It", *The New York Times* (24 February 2022), https://www.nytimes.com/2021/02/24/us/politics/biden-jamal-khashoggi-saudi-arabia.html (accessed 24 May 2022).
78 US Department of the Treasury, Press Release, Treasury Sanctions the Saudi Rapid Intervention Force and former Deputy Head of Saudi Arabia's General Intelligence Presidency for roles in the murder of journalist Jamal Khashoggi (21 February 2021), https://home.treasury.gov/news/press-releases/jy0038 (accessed 25 May 2022).
79 US Department of State, "Revocation of the Terrorist Destination of Ansarallah" (21 February 2021), https://www.state.gov/revocation-of-the-terrorist-designations-of-ansarallah/ (accessed 26 May 2022).
80 The White House, "Remarks by President Biden on America's Place in the World" (4 February 2021), https://www.whitehouse.gov/briefing-room/speeches-remarks/2021/02/04/remarks-by-president-biden-on-americas-place-in-the-world/ (accessed 22 May 2022).
81 The White House, "Letter to the Speaker of the House and President Pro Tempore of the Senate Regarding the War Powers Report" (7 December 2021), https://www.whitehouse.gov/briefing-room/statements-releases/2021/12/07/letter-to-the-speaker-of-the-house-and-president-pro-tempore-of-the-senate-regarding-the-war-powers-report-2/ (accessed 24 May 2022).
82 Ibid.
83 Ibid.
84 Ali Harb, "Is US Still Involved in Yemen War? Biden's Envoy Says He Doesn't Know", *Middle East Eye* (21 April 2021), https://www.middleeasteye.net/news/yemen-war-us-still-involved-biden-envoy-says-does-not-know (accessed 23 May 2022).
85 Sheren Khalel, "'Enables UAE's Reckless Conduct': Anti-War Advocates Slam $23bn US Arms Sale", *Middle East Eye* (14 April 2021), https://www.middleeasteye.net/news/biden-uae-arms-sale-23bn-denounced (accessed 23 May 2022).
86 US Government Accountability Office 2022.
87 Anelle R. Sheline and Bruce Riedel, "Biden's Broken Promise on Yemen", *Brookings* (16 September 2021), https://www.brookings.edu/blog/order-from-chaos/2021/09/16/bidens-broken-promise-on-yemen/ (accessed 23 May 2022).
88 Defense Security Cooperation Agency, https://www.dsca.mil/press-media/major-arms-sales
89 Fearon 1994.
90 Jennifer Stenihauer, Marj Mazetti, and Julie Hirchfield Davis, "Congress Votes to Override Obama Veto on 9/11 Victims Bill", *The New York Times* (28 September 2016), https://www.nytimes.com/2016/09/29/us/politics/senate-votes-to-override-obama-veto-on-9–11-victims-bill.html. The Trump administration argued that they were not able to release documents in order to protect sources and means; President Biden did release a heavily redacted

version of a previously classified document in September 2021, but the document adds only circumstantial evidence without any clear evidence of wrongdoing on the kingdom's part. See Eric Tucker, "FBI Releases Newly Declassified Record on the Sept. 11 Attacks", *AP News*, Associated Press (12 September 2021), https://apnews.com/article/9-11-saudi-arabia-fbi-declassified-86eec32f1b5b2ad7c9ba6bfbb98a4adb
91 Bernd Kaussler and Glenn Hastedt (2012). *US Foreign Policy Towards the Middle East: The Realpolitik of Deceit*. Routledge, p. 70.
92 Anne Applebaum, "Trump's Bizarre and Un-American Visit to Saudi Arabia", *The Washington Post* (21 May 2017), https://www.washingtonpost.com/news/global-opinions/wp/2017/05/21/trumps-bizarre-and-un-american-visit-to-saudi-arabia/ (accessed 5 May 2022).
93 Katja Kleinberg and Benjamin Fordham. "Don't Know Much about Foreign Policy: Assessing the Impact of "Don't Know" and "No Opinion" Responses on Inferences about Foreign Policy Attitudes", *Foreign Policy Analysis* 14 (3): 429–48.
94 Interview with author.
95 Ibid.
96 US Government Accountability Office 2022.
97 Ibid.
98 Ibid. Defense Security and Cooperation Agency, "Intended Sales to Saudi Arabia via Foreign Military Sales" (22 May 2017), https://www.dsca.mil/news-media/news-archive/fact-sheet-intended-sales-saudi-arabia-foreign-military-sales (accessed 12 July 2022).
99 US Government Accountability Office 2022.
100 Ibid.
101 Interview with author.
102 Ibid.
103 Interview with author.
104 Interview with author.
105 Navanti Report, Native Prospector, Yemen-Incident Tracker (18–24 November 2019), p. 5.
106 Navanti Report, Incident Tracker, Report # 245 (12–18 October 2020), p. 4.
107 Navanti Report, Houthi ACW and UAV Capabilities (17 December 2020), p. 3. It is important to note that the Yemeni military has been stockpiling missiles for decades. Tribal sheikhs and the Republican Guards too have sophisticated arsenal of missiles. Interview with author.
108 Interview with author.
109 Navanti Reports, *Native Prospector: Yemen, Executive Summary: Houthi ACW and UAV Capabilities* (17 December 2020), p. 1.
110 Ibid.
111 Navanti Report, Houthi ACW and UAV Capabilities (17 December 2020), p. 3.
112 Interview with author.
113 Navanti, Yemen: Incident Tracker, Report # 255 (21–27 December 2020), p. 5.
114 Accounts by the US Navy and the Saudi-led Coalition indicated that cross border smuggling from Iran into Yemen continued throughout the war.

While naval interdictions managed to disrupt some smuggling operations, the largely unmonitored beaches in Yemen provided extensives cover for smuggling. Native Prospector, Yemen: Incident Tracker (2–8 December 2019), p. 5.
115 Navanti Report, Houthi ACW and UAV Capabilities (17 December 2020), p. 3; Aziz el-Yaakoubi and Maha el-Dahan, "Saudi Aramco Petroleum Storage Site Hit by Houthi Attack, Fire Erupts", *Reuters* (26 March 2022), https://www.reuters.com/world/middle-east/saudi-air-defences-destroy-houthi-drones-state-tv-2022-03-25/ (accessed 29 May 2022); Alexander Cornwell, Alaa Siwlam, and Phil Stewart, "Yemen's Houthis Fail in Second Missile Attack on UAE", *Reuters* (24 January 2022), https://www.reuters.com/world/middle-east/uaes-defense-ministry-destroyed-2-houthi-ballistic-missiles-wam-2022-01-24/ (accessed 29 May 2022).
116 This graph stacks events identified by ACLED as "disrupted weapons use" atop the combined number of air/drone strikes and missile or artillery strikes launched by Houthi forces against targets within Saudi Arabia. Because the disrupted weapons use category also includes landmine and IED explosions, accidents, and others, disrupted attacks are coded manually using ACLED's event notes to ensure that all attacks represented were ranged attacks.
117 Navanti Report, Incident Tracker, Report # 263 (1–7 March 2021), p. 4.
118 Ibid.
119 Native Prospector, Yemen, Incident Tracker (25 November–December 2019), p. 5; Fabian Hinz, https://twitter.com/fab_hinz/status/1231603527086047233 (accessed 3 June 2022).
120 Navanti Report, Incident Tracker, Report # 263 (1–7 March 2021) p. 4.
121 Navanti, Yemen: Incident Tracker, Report # 255 (21–27 December 2020), p. 5.
122 Interview with author.
123 Interview with author.
124 Interview with author.
125 Houthi propaganda, focused on emphasizing grievances against the Yemeni Government and the Saudi-led Coalition and tried to shift blame away from Houthi governance failures. Native Prospector, Yemen, Executive Summary: Houthi Propaganda Assessment, Part III, Report # 253 (22 October 2020), p. 1.
126 The target audiences to gauge receptiveness for counter-Houthi messaging were surveyed across eight Houthi controlled governorates, as well as Sana'a capital municipality. A total of 1,008 (870 male and 121 female) surveys were conducted. We caution against overinterpretation of these results. The sample is not representative of the Yemeni population at large (especially with regard to the gender), and there is likely a selection effect related to the duration of Houthi territorial control and the likelihood that those with the strongest anti-Houthi sentiments would have left if possible. Navanti, Houthi Propaganda Assessment, Part II Report # 253 (22 October 2020), p. 13.
127 Ibid.
128 Ibid, p. 8.
129 Among Zaidis who did not affirmatively view the Houthis as representatives of the Zaidi sect (n = 276), 155, or 56%, were aged 15–35.

Further, 50% of Zaidi respondents did not express an active desire to join the front lines. Among that subset, 53% were aged 15–35. Similarly, a smaller minority of Zaidi respondents (33%) opposed or were indecisive about financially supporting the Houthi war effort. Moreover, respondents with an undergraduate degree were slightly more likely to hold very negative views of Iran, compared with the overall survey population. Zaidis in the greater Sana'a area also viewed Iran much less favorably than the surveyed Zaidi population overall (12% vs. 39%), ibid, p. 11.
130 Navanti, Southern Perceptions, Socotra Governorate, Report # 221 (12 March 2020), p. 2.
131 Based on 120 surveys. Navanti, Southern Perceptions, Socotra Governorate, Report # 221 (12 March 2020), p. 9.
132 Ibid.
133 Native Prospector, Yemen: Perceptions of Political Actors: Amran Governorate (3 October 2019), p. 3, 5.
134 Ibid.

6 Conclusion

From the onset of the civil war, Yemen's domestic political fabric was not only a formula for a protracted struggle over control of the state but also effectively triggered the two most powerful Middle East powers into supporting respective allied groups. The strive for regional dominance between Saudi Arabia and Iran would condemn Yemenis to suffer through the world's worst humanitarian crisis. By March 2022, over two-thirds of the population, or 23.4 million people, including 12.0 million children were in need of humanitarian assistance according to UNICEF. Over 17 million people were in need of food assistance.[1] In 2022, approximately 73% of over four million people displaced in Yemen were women and children.[2]

By all accounts, the eight year-long war coupled with the economic blockade of the country and the COVID-19 pandemic constituted the region's most protracted political, humanitarian, and developmental crisis. Our research has shown that the internationalization of the civil war not only prolonged the conflict but also ultimately made it more destructive.

A Houthi-run government that would be close to Iran was an unacceptable scenario to Saudi Arabia, and therefore caused Riyadh to form a regional coalition and launch the intervention in 2015. As far as Saudi motivations were concerned, a member of the US intelligence used the Vietnam analogy to describe both foreign policy determinants and outcome: the Saudis had to draw a line into the sand after Houthis took power, but ended up being bogged down in an unwinnable war.[3] While such realist thinking effectively compelled Saudis into the military intervention, it was exacerbated by Crown Prince Mohammed Bin Salman's expectation that a reinstatement of the Yemen government would be swift. Ironically, much like the decision-making surrounding Nasser's 1962 Yemen intervention, Saudis lacked strategy, military competence, and political acumen to unify Yemenis by force and proxy.

DOI: 10.4324/9781003262602-6

After eight years of war, Saudi objectives of destroying the Houthi movement and reinstalling the Hadi government remained elusive. Saudi Arabia's sophisticated weapons arsenal never translated into effective statesmanship nor helped the Saudi leadership to politically engineer a new central government in the country capable of governing and yielding a monopoly of violence. Our research has shown that Saudi and coalition air attacks against targets in Yemen would prove to be the conflict's most destructive feature. As far as the proxy war literature is concerned, Saudi Arabia's role was also rather unique because the country was an active belligerent in the conflict, and also acted as a proxy to the United States as well as was a patron to the Hadi government. Saudi objectives were maximalist in that they sought the reinstatement of the Hadi government that had ruled from exile in Riyadh since 2015. The Hadi government, therefore, became a Saudi proxy and was closely tied to both Saudi interests and demands.

However, the Iranian government primarily entered the war in order to "bait and bleed" Saudi resources. Support for Houthis was meant to balance against Saudi Arabia rather than politically engineer a Houthi-dominated government, though it certainly favored such an outcome. Unlike Saudi Arabia, Iran entered the war covertly. By all accounts, Iran succeeded in dragging Saudis into a protracted conflict while simultaneously accusing Riyadh of waging a war of aggression against its weaker neighbor. Without the steady supply of weapons including missiles and drones, Houthis would not have been able to continue their fight. Most importantly to Iranian leaders, the use of long-range weapons put Saudi Arabia on the defensive, effectively bringing the war onto Saudi soil. The attack on oil installations and airports by proxy allowed Iran's leaders to expose Saudi vulnerabilities. As communicated by the Panel of Experts to the UN Security Council in 2019:

> Beginning in August 2018, the Panel began noting the deployment of extended-range unmanned aerial vehicles with a range that would allow the Houthi forces to strike targets deep into Saudi Arabia and the United Arab Emirates. Based on the evidence available, the Panel observed that, unlike in 2015 and 2016 when the Houthi forces used complete or partially assembled weapons systems supplied from abroad, such as extended-range short-range ballistic missiles, they now increasingly rely on imports of high-value components, which are then integrated into locally assembled weapons systems, such as the extended-range unmanned aerial vehicles. The Panel is continuing to investigate whether the Houthis are assisted in the process by foreign experts.[4]

To decision-makers in Tehran, prolonging the war without attempting to impose any particular political framework for Yemen was an end in itself. While Houthis were technically Iran's proxies in their geopolitical strife against Saudi Arabia, Houthis enjoyed a good amount of autonomy in both decision-making and dependency, making the Iran-Houthi partnership more symbiotic compared to the hierarchical relationship between the Saudi and Yemeni governments. Ultimately, Iranian political support and weapon deliveries for Houthis coupled with the IRGC's extensive asymmetrical warfare experience decisively shifted the military balance to the Houthi's favor. Iran's key input was the continuous weapons transfers as well as fuel, ensuring that Houthis never faced any supply disruptions. While the coalition and the US Navy patrolled the Gulf of Aden and attempted to enforce the weapons embargo, the Houthi war economy primarily relied on illicit trade from Iran. Houthis also would not have been able to maintain territory without Tehran's backing. To Iran, material and political support for Houthis proved an effective and low-cost strategy in bogging down the Saudis into a lengthy, protracted conflict, draining both Saudi resources and the political will to meet its maximalist objectives. Reflecting on respective strategies, a member of the US military intelligence community in the Yemeni theater observed that Tehran's advantage in this proxy war was that Iran was able to leverage its economy to political militaries like the IRGC while Saudi Arabia leverages its wealth almost entirely into the economy.[5] This meant Saudis entered a war without any operational and tactical experience while the Iranian government was able to effectively and largely covertly supply and advise their surrogate in a prolonged conflict. By all accounts, Saudi power was no match for Iran's battlefield experience and willingness to share trenches with who they considered allies rather than just mere proxies.

The role of the United States as the "super patron" in this proxy conflict was instrumental in that it provided Saudi Arabia with weapons and effectively unconditional political support. With Houthis being seen as part of Iran's regional "threat network" by three US administrations, support for Saudi Arabia was meant to balance against Iran. Our data showed that Saudis conducted 24,399 air strikes between March 2015 and May 2022. The Yemen Human Security Map that was created as part of this research visualizes the deadly frequency of Saudi air strikes as well as the geographic coverage of those attacks. As the map shows, nowhere in Yemen were civilians safe from those air attacks.[6] Our data also indicated that US continuous weapons transfers to Saudi Arabia were crucial for these operations. Likewise, for US exports, this meant that the DoD administered $54 billion of military support to Saudi

Arabia and the UAE between 2015 and 2021. The US military support consisted of both defense articles and defense services, which included training to reduce civilian harm. The sales of defense articles included helicopters, missiles, and small diameter bombs.[7] However, as the only external patron which is a democracy, the United States faced the most direct audience cost with regards to the war's civilian death count and its patron's adherence to international humanitarian law. Notwithstanding respective bipartisan resolutions by Congress demanding for both President Trump and President Biden to end US military involvement in Yemen and support for the Saudi-led coalition, both administrations effectively provided a veneer of political legitimacy to Saudi Arabia's war efforts. Neither Obama nor his two successors were able or willing to exert any influence over the kingdom. Training that was given to the Saudi and UAE armed forces did not result in reducing civilian harm during sorties. All three US administrations allowed Saudi rulers to engage in practices that the United States would have condemned other countries for doing. Rather, embedding US military advisers in Saudi command structures helped Saudi forces improve operational capabilities without attaching any conditionalities with respect to international humanitarian law. In line with proxy war literature, it was a strategy that allowed US deniability for both alleged war crimes and mounting civilians deaths while simultaneously helping a proxy to continue its war efforts. While candidate Biden campaigned on changing US-Saudi relations because of the Khashoggi assassination, vowing "We [are] going to, in fact, make them pay the price, and make them, in fact, the pariah that they are",[8] the changed geopolitical landscape following Russia's invasion of Ukraine in early 2022 forced President Biden to visit Riyadh in July of of that year in order to strengthen bilateral relations.

Unlike proxy wars in Iraq and Syria whose volatile factional societal fabric were vulnerable to Saudi and Iranian involvements, the war in Yemen never turned into a sectarian conflict. For the most part, the struggle remained confined over control of the state with belligerents managing to keep their respective external backers' identity politics at bay. While Houthi rule resulted in some cultural changes in those territories they controlled, and all belligerents are being accused of war crimes, Yemen's tribal landscape prevented both patrons from demarcating the war along sectarian lines. While tribal power structures allowed for shifting alliances and truces during the conflict, they also present the war-torn country with its most likely path toward peace and national reconciliation. Tribal elders rely on a century-old tribal system of conflict resolution to arbitrage disputes and tensions between communities and enforce accountability and transparency amidst government failures. While the UN ceasefire provides for a workable roadmap toward peace, the most critical variable remains how tribes could both help administer transitional justice and decouple external actors from the major belligerent parties. The country's political realities and balance of power created by the conflict suggest that Houthis will minimally have stake in a future government if not full control. It will be up to the tribes to ensure neither Iran nor Saudi Arabia will act as a spoiler to peace, and help create a platform where crimes committed by all sides will be recognized.[9] Reflecting on the collective sense of loss and experienced trauma by every Yemeni, a member of the political elite considers the tribal sheikhs' political realism as the way forward to establish legitimacy, order, and stability, calling them "so pragmatic that it would have humbled Bismarck".[10] It is seen by many observers and stakeholders as the only way to overcome divisions and stop outside interference.

Notes

1 UNICEF, "Yemen-Humanitarian Situation Report Yemen" (March 2022), https://www.unicef.org/documents/yemen-humanitarian-situation-report-31-march-2022 (accessed 12 July 2022).
2 UNFP, "Yemen: The World's Largest Humanitarian Crisis" (November 2021), https://www.unfpa.org/yemen (accessed 12 July 2022).
3 Interview with author.
4 Letter dated January 25, 2019 from the Panel of Experts on Yemen addressed to the President of the Security Council - Final report of the Panel of Experts on Yemen (S/2019/83) [EN/AR], https://reliefweb.int/report/yemen/letter-dated-25-january-2019-panel-experts-yemen-addressed-president-security-council (accessed 12 July 2022).
5 Interview with author.
6 Bernd Kaussler, "Yemen Human Security Map" (Fall 2020), https://sites.lib.jmu.edu/yemen-human-security-project/?_ga=2.208617170.1334172540.1658334659-1738833869.1632065740 (accessed 12 July 2022).
7 Government Accountability Office, "Yemen: State and DOD Need Better Information on Civilian Impacts of U.S. Military Support to Saudi Arabia and the United Arab Emirates" (15 June 2022), https://www.gao.gov/products/gao-22-105988 (accessed 12 July 2022).
8 Oliver Knox, "Biden's Saudi Trip Isn't the Outlier. His 'Pariah' Comment Was". *The Washington Post* (15 June 2022), https://www.washingtonpost.com/politics/2022/06/15/bidens-saudi-trip-isnt-outlier-his-pariah-comment-was/ (accessed July 20, 2022).
9 Tarek Radwan, "Rethinking Transitional Justice in Yemen", *Atlantic Council* (3 February 2017), https://www.atlanticcouncil.org/blogs/menasource/rethinking-transitional-justice-in-yemen/ (accessed 28 July 2022).
10 Interview with author.

Index

Aden 3, 33, 34, 38, 39, 41, 42, 52–56, 58, 59, 63, 81, 82, 94, 121; battle of Aden 3, 38, 39
Afghanistan 2, 5, 24, 30, 32, 53, 64, 75, 109
Al-Jawf 57, 58, 105; Al-Jawf offensive 57–58
Al Qaeda in the Arabian Peninsula (AQAP) 31, 32, 34, 40, 53, 83, 85, 106
Ansar Allah (*see* Houthi)
Arab Spring 1, 3, 23, 25, 37, 64
Aramco 51–52, 58, 103, 104, 105
Armed Conflict Location and Event Data Project (ACLED) 3, 4, 38, 41, 62, 80, 95, 103

Bahrain 33, 37, 41, 77, 87
bait and bleed 3, 15, 31, 76, 86, 120
Biden, Joseph R. 4, 5, 32, 59, 60, 77, 84, 85, 93–97, 107, 108, 122
bin Salman, Mohammed 38, 43, 75, 85–88, 93
Blinken, Anthony 60
Bush, George W. 24, 30, 97

civilian victimization 3, 17, 33, 38, 48, 76, 89, 90, 92, 99, 122
coalition (*see* Saudi-Led Coalition)
Coronavirus 57, 58
COVAX 58; vaccines 58

drone (*see* unmanned aerial vehicles (UAV))

Egypt 25, 28, 33, 37, 86, 87

foreign military sales (FMS) 95, 99

General People's Congress (GPC) 1, 2, 40, 42, 43, 108

Hadi, Abd-Rabbu Mansour 1–3, 10, 16, 31–33, 37–39, 41, 43, 47, 50, 52–56, 58, 59, 75, 79–82, 96, 108, 109, 120; relations with the Coalition 3, 31, 37, 47, 52–54, 82, 120
Hodeidah 8, 12, 44, 45–50, 55, 61, 63, 76, 92; battle of Hoieidah 45–50, 92
Houthi 2–4, 8, 9, 12, 13, 16–18, 27–34, 37–55, 57–62, 64, 75, 79, 84, 85, 87, 89, 92–94, 99–110, 119–23; access to Iranian weaponry 8, 17, 29, 31, 32, 37, 38, 47, 52, 59, 60, 100–102, 105, 106, 108, 121; foreign terrorist designation 59–61; history of 2, 28, 100; military capabilities 8, 17, 18, 32, 37, 40, 45–47, 50–52, 59, 87, 89, 101–7; military engagements 4, 8, 29, 33, 37–40, 42–44, 46, 48, 50–52, 57, 58, 60, 61, 87, 92, 99, 101, 102, 105, 107, 120; relations with Iran 4, 8, 25, 26, 32, 33, 47, 51, 59, 62, 64, 78, 94, 99–101, 107, 121; relations with Saleh 2, 3, 38, 42, 43
Human Rights Watch (HRW) 44, 47, 85, 111

Hussein, Saddam 2, 24, 25, 30, 32, 84

improvised explosive devices (IED) 92, 102
International Crisis Group 54
international humanitarian law 79, 83, 84, 89, 92, 122
Iran 3, 4, 8, 9, 17, 23–34, 37, 38, 41, 42, 46, 47, 50–52, 54, 56, 59, 60, 62, 64, 75, 76, 78, 79, 84–90, 94, 99–107, 119–23
Iran Threat Network 31, 32; Quds Force 33, 56, 101, 102; relations with Hezbollah 26, 27, 31, 101, 109; relations with Houthi (*see* Houthi-relations with Iran); relations with Saudi Arabia 4, 23, 26, 60, 75, 107, 123; rivalry with Saudi Arabia 25, 26, 31, 62, 75, 105; sanctions against 31, 93; weapons transfers to Houthis (*see* Houthi-relations with Iran-access to Iranian weaponry)
Iran-Iraq War 32, 84, 101
Iraq 3, 5, 24–25, 28, 30, 32, 56, 64, 75, 79, 83, 107, 122; invasion of Iraq (2003) 3, 23, 24, 30
Islamic Revolutionary Guard Corps (IRGC) 30, 33, 64, 78, 101, 121
Islamic State (ISIS) 26, 27, 32, 34, 64, 83, 85, 94, 98

Khashoggi, Jamal 59, 62, 76, 88, 89, 93, 97, 122
Kushner, Jared 86, 87

Libya 3, 5, 7, 23, 25, 32, 64, 75

Marib 54, 57, 58, 62, 63, 105
Mattis, James 87, 89
Mnuchin, Steven 86
Muslim Brotherhood 2, 53, 87, 107

Obama, Barack H. 4, 30, 32, 84–86, 96, 97, 108, 122
offshore balancing 4, 32, 33, 46, 76, 84, 86, 97, 103
Operation Decisive Storm 3, 37–39
Operation Golden Victory 46

Patron 3, 4, 7–15, 17, 18, 23, 26, 30–32, 38, 41–42, 54, 57, 75–77, 79, 84, 85, 88, 89, 94, 99, 100, 102, 107–9, 120–22
Pompeo, Mike 56, 58, 59, 84
Proxy 3–15, 17, 18, 23–28, 30–34, 38, 42, 43, 59, 75–78, 83–86, 90, 94, 96–98, 100, 102, 105, 107–10, 119–22

Qatar 25, 26, 33, 37, 76, 87, 88; blockade 12, 31, 87, 88, 95, 96, 119

Russia 5, 23, 25–27, 85, 105, 122

Saleh, Ali Abdullah 1–3, 16, 29, 38, 42–44, 85
Saleh, Tareq 43, 44
Sana'a 2, 29, 37, 38, 42–44, 48, 51, 52, 54, 57, 61, 108, 109
Saudi Arabia 1–4, 8, 11, 13, 23–34, 37–44, 46, 47, 50–52, 54–62, 64, 75–105, 107–10, 119–23; alleged war crimes 13, 49, 59, 93, 98; border conflict 40, 41, 47, 51, 56, 57, 62, 77, 78, 84, 87, 100, 104, 105; break with UAE 4, 14, 41, 43, 53, 54, 62, 76, 77; relations with Hadi (*see* Hadi, Abd-Rabbu Mansour - relations with the Coalition); weapons transfers (*see* United States of America-relations with Saudi Arabia - weapons sales to Saudi Arabia)
Saudi-Led Coalition 2–4, 7–10, 12–16, 18, 31, 33, 37, 38, 40–50, 52–55, 57, 59, 61, 62, 76–80, 82–85, 87, 88, 90–92, 94–96, 100–103, 105, 108–10, 119–22; airstrikes 13, 26, 27, 31, 34, 38–40, 44, 45, 47, 63, 79, 80, 91, 96, 99, 104, 105, 120, 121; relations with Hadi (*see* Hadi, Abd-Rabbu Mansour-relations with the Coalition)
Soleimani, Qasem 56, 79
Southern Transitional Council (STC) 16, 34, 41, 53–56, 58, 82, 106, 108, 109
Stockholm Agreement 49, 76

Syria 3, 5, 23, 26–27, 32, 64, 75, 79, 83, 107, 122

Taliban 24, 64
third party intervention 3–11, 13–18, 23–32, 37, 38, 42, 44, 45, 55, 62, 64, 76–79, 82, 93, 107, 119
Tillerson, Rex 87, 98
tribes 1–3, 18, 34, 40, 42, 57, 62, 81, 83, 105–7, 109, 122, 123
Trump, Donald J. 4, 13, 23, 32, 44, 51, 56, 59, 77, 84–90, 93, 95, 96, 98, 99, 107, 110, 122
Turkey 23, 25–27, 105

Ukraine 5, 26, 87, 122; invasion of Ukraine 122
United Arab Emirates 4, 13, 25, 31, 33, 37, 41, 43, 44, 46–48, 50–56, 59, 62, 75–77, 80–84, 86, 87, 91, 92, 95, 98–103, 108–10, 120, 122, 123; break with Saudi Arabia (*see* Saudi Arabia - break with UAE); weapons transfers (*see* United States of America - weapons sales to UAE)
United Nations 1, 3, 4, 38, 44, 45, 47, 49, 51, 52, 56, 58, 60, 83; Special Envoy to Yemen 45, 58–60, 95; UNICEF 3, 4, 119, 123; United Nations Security Council 1, 39, 49, 51, 52, 58, 59, 83, 91, 120, 123
United States of America 2–5, 10, 13, 23, 27, 28, 30–34, 38, 44, 49, 56, 59, 60, 62, 64, 75–77, 79, 84–99, 107, 108, 110, 120–23; Central Command (CENTCOM) 80, 88–92; Congress 1, 10, 40, 60, 76, 77, 87–91, 93, 94, 97, 98, 108, 110, 122; Defense Security Cooperation Agency (DCSA) 77, 110; Department of Defense 79, 89, 92, 98, 99; Department of State 60, 78, 79, 85, 89–92, 95; Department of the Treasury 93; relations with Saudi Arabia 86, 88, 89, 97, 122; as a super patron 4, 23, 32, 38, 59, 75, 76, 79, 85, 88, 94, 99, 108, 121; weapons sales to Saudi Arabia 62, 77, 78, 89, 99, 108, 110, 121; weapons sales to UAE 77, 95, 110
unmanned aerial vehicles (UAV) 52, 60, 93, 101, 102, 103, 104, 105, 120

Votel, Joseph 89, 90

Wahhabism 29, 98
war crimes 3, 9, 13, 38, 47, 48, 49, 59, 61, 76, 77, 79, 89, 91, 92, 97, 99, 107, 122, 123
War Powers Act 76, 77, 88, 94, 97
weapons transfer 8, 10, 12, 17, 52, 60, 77, 89, 95, 96, 98, 99, 106, 110, 121

Yemen, Republic of 1–5, 8, 10, 12, 13, 15, 16, 18, 23, 24, 27–34, 37, 38, 40–47, 49, 50, 52–64, 75–110, 119–23; Cabinet 52–54, 56, 59, 80–82, 94; history of 23, 24, 27, 28, 30, 43, 77, 100, 106; Supreme Judiciary Council 1; Supreme Political Council 42; Supreme Revolutionary Committee 48

For Product Safety Concerns and Information please contact our EU representative GPSR@taylorandfrancis.com
Taylor & Francis Verlag GmbH, Kaufingerstraße 24, 80331 München, Germany

www.ingramcontent.com/pod-product-compliance
Lightning Source LLC
Chambersburg PA
CBHW051753230426
43670CB00012B/2270